American English

Personal Best

C1 Advanced

Student's Book and Workbook combined edition A

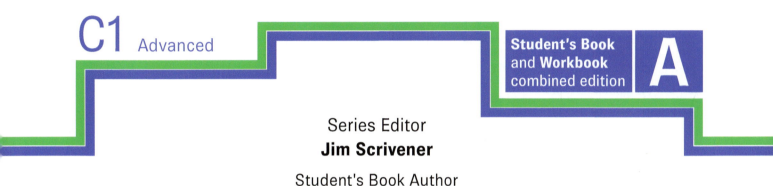

Series Editor
Jim Scrivener

Student's Book Author
Bess Bradfield

Workbook Authors
Elizabeth Walters and Kate Woodford

STUDENT'S BOOK CONTENTS

		LANGUAGE			SKILLS	
		GRAMMAR	PRONUNCIATION	VOCABULARY		
1 What matters		■ the present: simple, continuous, and perfect aspects ■ adding emphasis (1): cleft sentences	■ /s/ and /z/ ■ intonation in cleft sentences	■ attitudes and emotions ■ abstract nouns	READING ■ an article about Gregory Porter's family values ■ dealing with non-literal language ■ past habits	SPEAKING ■ paraphrasing ■ using fillers **PERSONAL BEST** ■ a discussion about our most important possessions
1A Formula for happiness	p4					
1B Family values	p6					
1C The right decision	p8					
1D What would you save?	p10					
2 Live better		■ modal verbs (1) and modal-like forms ■ modal verbs (2): advanced forms	■ linking modal-like forms with *to* ■ stress patterns with modal verb forms	■ health and medical treatment ■ life skills and well-being ■ verbs and nouns with the same form	LISTENING ■ a video looking at stress-relieving activities ■ understanding attitude and opinion ■ the disappearing /ə/ in fast speech	WRITING ■ giving constructive criticism ■ uses of *quite* **PERSONAL BEST** ■ a review of a course
2A Health fact, health fiction	p12					
2B My quest for quiet time	p14					
2C Missing out?	p16					
2D Highly recommended	p18					

1 and **2** — REVIEW and PRACTICE p20

		GRAMMAR	PRONUNCIATION	VOCABULARY		
3 Looking back		■ past time ■ comparison	■ weak forms of *had* and *been* ■ /ə/ sound	■ change and time ■ expressions with *come* and *go*	READING ■ an article about the life of Helen Keller ■ understanding text structure and organization ■ narrating the future from the past	SPEAKING ■ reminiscing ■ fixing errors **PERSONAL BEST** ■ telling a story about something that happened to you
3A Sign of the times	p22					
3B A remarkable life	p24					
3C Delicious discoveries	p26					
3D The time of my life	p28					
4 Success and failure		■ verb patterns (1): infinitives and -*ing* forms ■ adding emphasis (2): inversion and *do/does/did*	■ linking after *to* ■ sentence stress: emphatic *do/does/did*	■ success and failure ■ expressions with *make* and *take* ■ idioms	LISTENING ■ a video about making mistakes ■ understanding reasons and outcomes ■ linking consonants and vowels	WRITING ■ writing a report ■ formal linkers **PERSONAL BEST** ■ a report about your progress
4A Brilliant failure	p30					
4B Make more mistakes!	p32					
4C Making it big	p34					
4D Progress report	p36					

3 and **4** — REVIEW and PRACTICE p38

		GRAMMAR	PRONUNCIATION	VOCABULARY		
5 Entertain us!		■ ellipsis and substitution ■ noun phrases	■ strong and weak forms of *to* ■ word stress in compound nouns	■ tastes and opinions ■ verb suffixes	READING ■ three movie reviews ■ understanding tone ■ identifying the subject in long sentences	SPEAKING ■ speculating ■ using repetition **PERSONAL BEST** ■ a discussion about changes in your city
5A We know what you like	p40					
5B Simply a triumph	p42					
5C Standing out	p44					
5D Everything changes	p46					

Grammar practice **p94**   Vocabulary practice **p114**   Communication practice **p130**

Language App, unit-by-unit grammar and vocabulary games

WORKBOOK CONTENTS

		LANGUAGE			SKILLS	
		GRAMMAR	PRONUNCIATION	VOCABULARY		
1	**What matters** **1A** p2 **1B** p3 **1C** p4 **1D** p5	▪ the present: simple, continuous, and perfect aspects ▪ adding emphasis (1): cleft sentences	▪ /s/ and /z/ ▪ intonation in cleft sentences	▪ attitudes and emotions ▪ abstract nouns	**READING** ▪ dealing with non-literal language	**SPEAKING** ▪ paraphrasing
1	**REVIEW and PRACTICE** p6					
2	**Live better** **2A** p8 **2B** p9 **2C** p10 **2D** p11	▪ modal verbs (1) and modal-like forms ▪ modal verbs (2): advanced forms	▪ linking modal-like forms with *to* ▪ stress patterns with modal verb forms	▪ health and medical treatment ▪ life skills and well-being ▪ verbs and nouns with the same form	**LISTENING** ▪ understanding attitude and opinion	**WRITING** ▪ giving constructive criticism
2	**REVIEW and PRACTICE** p12					
3	**Looking back** **3A** p14 **3B** p15 **3C** p16 **3D** p17	▪ past time ▪ comparison	▪ weak forms of *had* and *been* ▪ /ə/ sound	▪ change and time ▪ expressions with *come* and *go*	**READING** ▪ understanding text structure and organization	**SPEAKING** ▪ reminiscing
3	**REVIEW and PRACTICE** p18					
4	**Success and failure** **4A** p20 **4B** p21 **4C** p22 **4D** p23	▪ verb patterns (1): infinitives and *-ing* forms ▪ adding emphasis (2): inversion and *do/does/did*	▪ linking after *to* ▪ sentence stress: emphatic *do/does/did*	▪ success and failure ▪ expressions with *make* and *take* ▪ idioms	**LISTENING** ▪ understanding reasons and outcomes	**WRITING** ▪ writing a report
4	**REVIEW and PRACTICE** p24					
5	**Entertain us** **5A** p26 **5B** p27 **5C** p28 **5D** p29	▪ ellipsis and substitution ▪ noun phrases	▪ strong and weak forms of *to* ▪ word stress in compound nouns	▪ tastes and opinions ▪ verb suffixes	**READING** ▪ understanding tone	**SPEAKING** ▪ speculating
5	**REVIEW and PRACTICE** p30					

Writing practice **p62**

3

UNIT 1

What matters

LANGUAGE the present: simple, continuous, and perfect aspects ■ attitudes and emotions

1A Formula for happiness

1 **A** In pairs, discuss the questions.
1 On a scale of one to ten, how happy a person are you in general?
2 If you're not feeling particularly happy, what do you do to lift your mood? Does it always work?

B Look at the verbs and expressions in the box. Which are associated with happiness?

> look on the bright side   be down to earth   feel down   cheer up   be over the moon

Go to Vocabulary practice: attitudes and emotions, page 114

2 A ▶ 1.3   In pairs, take "The science of happiness" quiz. Then listen and check.

The science of happiness

Scientists have been studying happiness for decades, and they're still making new discoveries about what makes us happy. How much do you know about happiness?

1 Eating chocolate cheers us up because it contains:
  a   large quantities of sugar.
  b   serotonin, the "love" chemical.
  c   tryptophan, which turns into serotonin.

2 When we feel down, we should:
  a   listen to slow, depressing songs.
  b   listen to upbeat, cheerful songs.
  c   not listen to music at all.

3 Which of the following activities makes us feel happier?
  a   binge-watching TV
  b   baking your favorite cakes
  c   eating your favorite cakes

4 For optimum happiness, how many hours should we sleep a night?
  a   six hours
  b   seven hours
  c   eight hours

5 What's the best temperature to be happy?
  a   approximately 14°C
  b   exactly 22°C
  c   approximately 30°C

6 What has the greatest effect on our overall happiness?
  a   pursuing pleasure
  b   feeling thankful
  c   being wealthy

B Which answer surprised you most?

3 ▶ 1.4   Complete the sentences with the correct form of the verbs in parentheses. Listen and check.
1 Tom, you _____ always _____ me from my work! (distract)
2 As a matter of fact, I _____ a little bit down lately. (feel)
3 I _____ to lots of salsa music these days. (listen)
4 Researchers _____ that sad songs actually lift our mood. (find)
5 When we _____ on doing a structured activity that's also pretty physical, we _____ focusing on how we feel. (concentrate, stop)
6 I usually only _____ six hours of sleep a night, though. (get)

4

the present: simple, continuous, and perfect aspects ■ attitudes and emotions   **LANGUAGE 1A**

4 Look at the verb forms in exercise 3. Match sentences 1–6 with aspects a–c below. Some verb forms have two aspects. Then read the Grammar box.

a simple _____ _____ _____   b continuous _____ _____ _____   c perfect _____ _____

> **Grammar** the present: simple, continuous, and perfect aspects
>
> **Simple present:**
> Spain **produces** 45% of all the olive oil in the world.
> We **commute** downtown by train.
>
> **Present continuous:**
> I'**m** just **finishing** an e-mail to my teacher.
> She'**s** always **making** me late!
>
> **Present perfect:**
> Real Madrid **has won** La Liga 33 times.
> I **haven't finished** my assignment yet.
>
> **Present perfect continuous:**
> I'**ve been trying** to connect to the Internet all day.
> He's out of breath because he'**s been jogging**.
>
> **Look!** The continuous aspect can indicate that an action is not necessarily completed:
> I've been reading a book about happiness.
> The perfect aspect connects the past to another point in time, in this case the present:
> I've lived in the suburbs for a year.

Go to Grammar practice: the present: simple, continuous, and perfect aspects, page 94

5 A ▶1.6 **Pronunciation:** /s/ and /z/ Listen to the sentences. Is the "s" in **bold** pronounced with an /s/ or a /z/ sound?

1 She'**s** been staying at a friend's house.
2 It'**s** been a long time since I've seen him.
3 He'**s** been working late again.
4 It'**s** ages until we go away on vacation.
5 She'**s** only just starting to write her assignment.
6 Jack'**s** been washing the car. He'**s** wet.

B ▶1.6 Listen again and repeat.

Go to Communication practice: Student A page 130, Student B page 141

6 A Complete the sentences with the correct present form of the verbs in the box.

play   get   check   give   lose   study   work   say

1 Your best friend _____ the job of her dreams!
2 Your neighbor _____ loud music for five hours. It's now 3 a.m.
3 Apparently, a colleague or classmate _____ something sarcastic about you.
4 You _____ at home all day, and you haven't spoken to anyone, not even your boss.
5 Your brother or sister _____ always _____ his or her phone during mealtimes.
6 Your favorite team _____ five games in a row this season.
7 You _____ eight hours a day recently, and your teacher often _____ you extra assignments.

B In pairs, discuss how you would feel and what you would do or say in the situations in exercise 6A.

7 In pairs, discuss the questions below.

1 Do you know anyone who always looks on the bright side of life, despite its setbacks? Who?
2 Do you know anyone who's been feeling down recently? Have you been able to cheer him/her up?
3 Do you think you've ever come across badly when meeting new people? What happened?
4 How conscientious a person are you, especially regarding your job or studies?
5 Which new activities have you thrown yourself into over the past few years? How are they going?
6 What's the most courageous thing that someone you know has ever done?
7 In your opinion, do women tend to be more open-minded than men, or is it the other way around?

Personal Best   Write a paragraph describing what your formula for happiness is.   5

1 SKILLS

READING dealing with non-literal language ■ past habits

1B Family values

1 **A** In pairs, tell your partner your most vivid memories from childhood.

B Read the introduction and the first paragraph of the text on page 7. Who is Gregory Porter? What is his most vivid memory from childhood?

2 Read the complete text. Are the sentences true (T) or false (F)? <u>Underline</u> the sections in the text that support your answers.

1 Gregory had a privileged upbringing. _____
2 His father played an important part in his childhood. _____
3 His brothers and sisters didn't get along well at all. _____
4 Gregory learned many important values from his mother. _____
5 He wasn't a natural risk-taker as a child. _____
6 Gregory has achieved what his mother wanted for him. _____

> **Skill** dealing with non-literal language
>
> **Writers sometimes use language non-literally, with a meaning that's different from the literal definition. You can often guess the meaning by looking for clues in the non-literal word or expression, and in the context around it.**
> - Identify the literal meaning of the word or expression. What part of speech is it?
> - Look at the sentences before and after the word or expression. What is this part of the text about? What or who does it refer to?
> - Now guess the non-literal meaning. Can you think of a synonym?

3 **A** Read the Skill box. Look at the <u>underlined</u> words and expressions in the text. Follow the steps in the Skill box for each of them.

B Now choose the correct definition for each word or expression.

1 **a** with help **b** without any help **c** while unmarried
2 **a** closely connected **b** having many hobbies **c** unconventional
3 **a** get exercise **b** do our fair share of work **c** do all the work
4 **a** on vacation **b** at work **c** away from home for work
5 **a** too small a space **b** a lot of fun **c** a difficult situation
6 **a** make someone forget **b** discuss **c** teach by repeating

> **Text builder** past habits
>
> **We use various structures to talk about actions and situations that happened repeatedly in the past.**
> Simple past: *She never **complained** – she just **got on with** it.*
> Past continuous: *Our washing machine **was always breaking down.***
> *would*: *By the end, everybody **would be laughing**.*
> *used to*: *My sisters **used to be** the gang leaders.*

4 Read the Text builder. What repeated actions or situations can you remember about Gregory's childhood?

5 Look at the text and find another example of each structure highlighted in the Text builder.

6 In pairs, discuss the questions below.

1 What did family life use to be like when you were young?
2 What do you think your family values are?
3 Who taught you your family values?
4 Which of these values have been the most useful so far in your life?

6

dealing with non-literal language ■ past habits   READING   SKILLS   1B

My family values: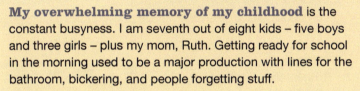
Gregory Porter

Grammy award-winning American singer and songwriter Gregory Porter is instantly recognizable, both for his velvet-smooth baritone and signature hat (the chin-straps hide scars from skin surgery). Porter's crossover jazz-pop hit "Liquid Spirit" became the most streamed jazz album in history, remixed by dance DJs and featured on soap opera soundtracks. But, as he tells journalist Sarah Ewing, he owes who he is today to his family.

My overwhelming memory of my childhood is the constant busyness. I am seventh out of eight kids – five boys and three girls – plus my mom, Ruth. Getting ready for school in the morning used to be a major production with lines for the bathroom, bickering, and people forgetting stuff.

Dad was largely absent. Mom did a great job of taking care of us all, [1]single-handedly. We were a very [2]tight-knit family, but we all had to [3]pull our weight. My sisters started to cook at nine and, being one of the youngest, I wanted in on it, too, so I began at six on potato-peeling duty, as French fries were my thing.

Mom had an incredible work ethic. She held down three jobs for much of her life to help support us, as an overnight nurse, a realtor, and a pastor. She never complained, she just got on with it. Oddly, I never remember her gone – she was always there when we needed her. I don't know how she managed it all with eight kids. Our washing machine was always breaking down. Even being [4]on the road 300 days a year, doing 250 shows, I don't think I'm working anywhere near as hard as my mother.

It was always [5]a tight squeeze wherever we lived. At one place, the laundry room was converted into a bedroom for us boys, but the hardest was when all eight of us and Mom were in a one-bed apartment in Los Angeles. One of us got chickenpox, and then we all did. Family mealtimes were always very sociable with us sitting as a group on the floor.

Adapted from theguardian.com

The underlying value Mom taught us was respect, everyone from strangers on the street to our elders. Having such a large family, she wanted to [6]drill these basic values of compassion, empathy, and mutual respect into us from a young age so she didn't have to micromanage us. It's an easy, simple message, but often difficult to achieve.

We tried not to fight, or at least get caught fighting, because Mom would make us go through an embarrassing ritual where she would get us to hug and then kiss each other. By the end, everybody would be laughing because we would be hamming it up.

I was pretty shy as a child. My sisters used to be the gang leaders, my brothers were the enforcers, and I was a tag-along. I liked staying safe, so I was always trying to keep my older brother Lloyd out of trouble, telling him off for being too risky and adventurous.

My mother gave me the courage to pursue music as a career on her deathbed. She became very ill when I was 21. I didn't want her to worry about my future. I wanted her to know I'd finish my degree. But she pushed me to follow my dream, even if it wasn't the safe option.

I'm now a dad myself (to son Demyan), and I want to be the opposite of my dad. I love being involved with him and letting him know I'm rooting for him, and will support him in whatever he does. Shouldn't every parent?

Personal Best — Write a paragraph about what you used to be like as a child.

7

1 LANGUAGE — adding emphasis (1): cleft sentences ■ abstract nouns

1C The right decision

1 In your opinion, what are the most important qualities for a good relationship with a friend, partner, or sibling? Choose from the words in the box and add your own ideas.

> sensitivity   generosity   reliability   tolerance   patience   wisdom   honesty

Go to Vocabulary practice: abstract nouns, page 115

2 Look at the picture below. What's happening? Read the text and check your answer.

3 Read the text again and choose the correct options 1–5.

The right decision?

In an act of brotherly love which made global headlines, the British athlete Alistair Brownlee sacrificed his chance of winning the silver medal in the final 700 meters of the 2016 World Triathlon Series in Mexico. The reason why he did it was to help his younger brother, Jonny, who was also competing in the final.

When Alistair spotted his brother leading in the last stretch of the race, he was full of [1]*pride / annoyance*. "I was thinking: this is perfect – Jonny's ahead of me. He's going to win the world title." In fact, it was Alistair who became the star of the race. As the hot sun blazed, Jonny started to sway. He also appeared confused, like he was losing [2]*awareness / patience* of his surroundings. What Jonny was experiencing was heatstroke – a very dangerous condition that can be fatal without swift treatment. Recognizing the symptoms, Alistair didn't hesitate. He put an arm around his brother and almost pushed him over the finish line. Medics then rushed Jonny to the hospital, where he made a full recovery. In the end, Jonny was awarded second place, and Alistair came in third. Jonny later thanked his brother for his [3]*tolerance / loyalty*. Alistair responded modestly, saying it was a decision he'd made instinctively.

What had motivated Alistair was concern for Jonny. "You can die from exertional heatstroke if you don't receive medical attention very quickly. And the medics are all at the end of the race." He added that their mom wouldn't have been happy if he'd left his little brother behind! Many people have applauded Alistair's moment of [4]*honesty / kindness*, but it's a controversial decision that's divided the athletic community. Some question the [5]*fairness / inconvenience* of the race result, and believe the pair should have been disqualified. So does Alistair still believe it was worth it? "Yeah, of course," he says. "He's going to have to pay me back though – that's for sure."

4 Do you think they both deserve their awards? Why/Why not?

5 A Look at the pairs of sentences below. How were the first sentences expressed in the text? Complete the second sentences and then check your answers.

1 He did it to help his younger brother.
   The reason why _____ to help his younger brother.
2 Alistair became the star of the race.
   It was _____ the star of the race.
3 Jonny was experiencing heatstroke.
   What _____ heatstroke.
4 Concern for Jonny had motivated Alistair.
   What _____ concern for Jonny.

B Look at the sentences in exercise 5A again. What is the effect of starting the second sentence with the words in **bold**? Choose the correct answer: a or b. Then read the Grammar box.

a   The information after the words in **bold** is emphasized.   b   The sentence is turned into a question.

adding emphasis (1): cleft sentences ■ abstract nouns   LANGUAGE   1C

Grammar — adding emphasis (1): cleft sentences

Adding emphasis with *It*:
It was my father who inspired me.
It's every Friday when we usually get together.

Adding emphasis with *What*:
What I really need is coffee.
What worries me most is climate change.

Adding emphasis with *The person who* ... , etc.:
The person who just called was my boss.
The thing that annoyed me most was the noise.
The reason why I came over was to give you a hand.
The place that I love the most is the beach.

Look! *What* ... and *The thing that* ... have the same meaning:
What I need is a long vacation. *The thing that I need* is a long vacation.

Go to Grammar practice: adding emphasis (1): cleft sentences, page 95

6 A 🔊 1.9 **Pronunciation:** intonation in cleft sentences Listen to the sentences. Pay attention to the falling intonation toward the end of the cleft clause.

1 **It was John** who showed the most tolerance and patience.
2 **It's the five-hour trip** that I find so unbearable.
3 **It's global warming** that worries me the most.
4 **It was January** when we went back to school.
5 **It was one of the neighbors** who broke the front door.
6 **It wasn't me** who ate the last slice of cheesecake.

B 🔊 1.9 Listen again and repeat.

7 A 🔊 1.10 Listen to the people talking about a decision. Complete the notes with a short phrase.

Tom

Tom's been offered a job as a ¹_____ . He'd like to take the job because he's always wanted to ² _____ . Tom's worried about Sylvia because she ³ _____ , and she just ⁴ _____ . One solution might be for Tom to ⁵ _____ every week.

Sarah

Amy wants to borrow ⁶ _____ from Sarah. Amy wants to go to the U.K. to visit ⁷ _____ . Sarah's worried because two years ago, Amy ⁸ _____ , but didn't ⁹ _____ . Now Sarah's worried about their ¹⁰ _____ .

Jake

Jake's father wants him to take over ¹¹ _____ , but Jake has always wanted to work as ¹² _____ . Ironically, ¹³ _____ encouraged him to study this field in college. Jake's upset now because ¹⁴ _____ is questioning Jake's ¹⁵ _____ to the family.

B In pairs, discuss what decision you think each person should make. Give reasons for your choice.

Go to Communication practice: Student A page 130, Student B page 141

8 Complete the sentences so they are true for you. In pairs, ask and answer questions about your sentences.

1 The decision that's been the trickiest for me to make was ...
2 The place that I've always dreamed of living some day is ...
3 Since I was young, all I've ever wanted to do is ...
4 What I need right now is ...
5 What the world needs right now is ...
6 The thing that fascinates me most about my program/career is ...
7 The people who I'd most like to invite over to dinner would be ...
8 All I want to do when I get back home is ...

Personal Best Write a paragraph about the best decision you've ever made.

1 SKILLS SPEAKING paraphrasing ■ using fillers

1D What would you save?

1 Discuss the questions in pairs.
1. What are your four most important possessions? Give reasons for your choices.
2. Are they items of practical importance, or do they have sentimental value?

2 ▶ 1.11 Watch or listen to the first part of a webshow called *Talking Zone*. Answer the questions.
1. What just happened in Ben and Abigail's building?
2. What item did Ben take with him?
3. What is Abigail's "burning building item"?

3 A ▶ 1.11 Choose the correct option to complete Ben and Abigail's conversation. Watch or listen again and check.

Abigail Is that your laptop?
Ben Yeah. Why?
Abigail Nothing. It's just interesting, that's all.
Ben What do you mean?
Abigail Sorry, let me ¹*repeat / rephrase* that. It's kind of revealing that your laptop is your burning building item.
Ben Um, I just grabbed it when the alarm went off. I don't know if it's my burning building item. Whatever that is.
Abigail What I ²*mean / want* by that is it says a lot about someone, doesn't it? What they'd think of saving if the building was on fire.
Ben OK, I ³*see / get* it. So you're ⁴*telling / saying* that it's like a test to see what it is that you value the most.

B Look at the conversation in exercise 3A. Which two expressions does Abigail use to clarify or emphasize what she means? Which expression does Ben use to check he has understood what Abigail means?

Conversation builder   paraphrasing

Rephrasing an idea to clarify or emphasize what you mean
Let me rephrase that …
So, what I mean is …
In other words …
What I mean by that is …
Or, to put it another way …
That is to say, …

Checking you've understood by rephrasing something
So, you're saying that …
So, what you mean is … . Is that right?
Let me see, so …
What I think you're saying is …
Oh, I see / I get it, so …
Let me get this straight.
So, the basic idea is …

4 A ▶ 1.11 Read the Conversation builder. Watch or listen again. Which other expressions from the builder do Ben and Abigail use?

B In pairs, discuss the question below. Use the expressions from the Conversation builder to clarify or emphasize what you mean, and to check what your partner has said.

Which of your possessions most reminds you of the following things, and why?
1. a family member
2. your childhood
3. an important event in your life
4. a great time you had with a close friend

paraphrasing ■ using fillers **SPEAKING** SKILLS **1D**

5 ▶ 1.12 Watch or listen to the second part of the show and answer the questions.
1 Which items of sentimental value do Ben and Abigail choose?
2 What reasons for choosing these items do they give?

6 ▶ 1.12 Order sentences a–g. Watch or listen again and check.

a ☐ **Abigail** That's a good question. I think I'd save my grandmother's ring, as well as my phone.
b ☐ **Ben** In a fire? I don't know. I've never really considered it before. But yeah, probably.
c ☐ **Abigail** Why?
d ☐ **Ben** It's, like, not the laptop that's important. It's everything that's on it. I mean, I've been working from home for nearly a year now, and everything is on that computer. It would be a huge inconvenience to lose it all.
e [1] **Abigail** Do you think you'd really save just your laptop?
f ☐ **Ben** What about you? Would you save one thing, or try to grab lots of stuff?
g ☐ **Abigail** Yeah. I see what you mean.

🔧 **Skill** using fillers

We use fillers to give us time to think and to avoid long pauses. Fillers can also be used to indicate that you haven't finished speaking so people don't interrupt you. Typical fillers include:
• words and expressions, e.g., *like, kind of, basically, you see, let's see, I mean, you know what I mean?*
• phrases when answering a question, e.g., *That's a good question … , I've never really considered it before … , Oh, that's a hard one …*
• sounds, e.g., *um* and *hmm*.
Be careful not to use too many fillers or you may sound hesitant and unsure.

7 A Read the Skill box. Which filler phrases in exercise 6 are used when answering a question?

B Complete the conversation with one word in each blank. The first letter is given for you. Practice the conversation with a partner, changing the information so it is true for you.

A If you could live anywhere, where would you live?
B Er … I've never ¹r_____ thought about it before. Do you mean anywhere in this country?
A No, I mean anywhere in the world.
B That's a ²h_____ one! Let's ³s_____ , hmm … maybe Australia. It looks beautiful.
A Yeah, but it's ⁴k_____ of … far away from everywhere else, do you ⁵k_____ what I mean?
B Yeah, but these days you can, ⁶l_____ , fly anywhere pretty easily. Anyway, what about you?
A I'd live in Paris. The most romantic city on earth!

Go to Communication practice: Student A page 131, Student B page 142

8 A PREPARE Plan your answers to the following questions.
1 Which item of sentimental value would you save first in an emergency?
2 If you had to choose between saving an item of practical importance and an item of sentimental value, which would you choose? Why?

B PRACTICE Discuss your answers in pairs. Use paraphrasing and fillers.

C PERSONAL BEST What information did you paraphrase? Did you use fillers? Repeat with a new partner.

Personal Best Write a conversation between you and a friend discussing what you would save in an emergency.

UNIT 2 Live better

LANGUAGE modal verbs (1) and modal-like forms ■ health and medical treatment

2A Health fact, health fiction

1 In pairs, discuss what advice you would give a friend who:
   1 suffers from **splitting headaches**.
   2 always seems to **pick up every bug** around.
   3 has a broken leg, which is **in a cast**.

   Go to Vocabulary practice: health and medical treatment, page 116

2 **A** Read the health advice headlines below. Do you think any of them are factually correct?

   a **Everyone should eat TEN portions of fruit and vegetables a day**

   b **Never miss breakfast – the most important meal**

   c **To stay in shape, you need to walk 10,000 steps a day!**

   d **Exercise is supposed to hurt. No pain, no gain!**

   e **Cold outside? Stay in, stay warm, and you'll stay well, too**

   B ▶ 2.3 Listen to a podcast about health advice and check your answers to exercise 2A. Which information surprised you the most?

3 **A** ▶ 2.3 Complete sentences 1–8 from the podcast with words from the box. Listen again and check.

   have to   need to   should   prepared to   managed to   'd better   likely to   supposed to

   1 Realistically, few of us are _____ achieve the target of ten portions a day.
   2 It doesn't matter if you were in a rush, and only _____ grab a cup of coffee for breakfast.
   3 If you're feeling dizzy or tired, you _____ rethink your eating habits urgently!
   4 We all _____ get enough exercise, but it's not necessary to count steps in order to stay in shape.
   5 If you need motivation to be more active, you really _____ get a pedometer.
   6 Personal trainers are _____ advise you about how to avoid pulling a muscle.
   7 Be _____ rest if you're injured – it's essential to give your injury time to heal.
   8 Exercising in the fresh air _____ boost your immunity to viruses, as it gets your heart and lungs working.

   B Match the modal forms in exercise 3A with functions a–h below. Then read the Grammar box.
   a necessity   _____
   b expected obligation   _____
   c ability to do something (with some difficulty)   _____
   d strong possibility   _____
   e strong probability   _____
   f strong recommendation   _____
   g strong advice or warning   _____
   h be willing to do something   _____

12

modal verbs (1) and modal-like forms ■ health and medical treatment   LANGUAGE   2A

📖 Grammar   modal verbs (1) and modal-like forms

Advice and recommendation:
You'**d better** change your habits.
You **have to** try this relaxation app!
I really **ought to** lose some weight.

Ability and willingness:
I **managed to** lose 10 kg. last year.
I'**m prepared to** give up desserts.

Possibility and speculation:
How long **is** the pain **likely to** last?
The symptoms **should** clear up soon.
This **may** help with your recovery.

Obligation and necessity:
You **need to** take this pill with water.
The pharmacist **is supposed to** give you advice.

Look! There are two negative forms of *need to*: *doesn't need to* and *needn't*. *Needn't* is more formal and is only used for immediate necessity, not general necessity:
He **doesn't need to/needn't** go to the hospital.
You **don't need to** pay for medical care in this country.

Go to Grammar practice: modal verbs (1) and modal-like forms, page 96

4 A ▶ 2.5   **Pronunciation:** linking modal-like forms with *to*   Listen to the sentences. What happens to the consonant sounds /t/ and /d/ before *to*?

1 You're not **supposed to** wake someone up if they're sleepwalking.
2 If you can **manage to** go running every day, you should.
3 Reading in low light is **likely to** damage your eyesight.
4 You should be **prepared to** wait for at least 30 minutes after a meal before swimming.
5 You don't really **need to** brush your teeth twice a day.
6 You **ought to** eat more carrots if you want to see in the dark.

B ▶ 2.5   Listen again and repeat.

5 In pairs, discuss which sentences in exercise 4A are good advice.

6 Rewrite sentences 1–5. Use between three and five words, including a word from the box.

better   manage   likely   need   prepared

1 Giving up all snacks isn't essential.
  You _____ all snacks.
2 I couldn't stick to the exercise regime.
  I _____ to the exercise regime.
3 Eating too much salt will probably cause high blood pressure.
  Eating too much salt _____ high blood pressure.
4 Losing her prescription will get you into trouble.
  You _____ her prescription or you'll get into trouble.
5 I refuse to let stress rule my life!
  I _____ stress rule my life!

Go to Communication practice: Student A page 131, Student B page 142

7 In pairs, discuss the questions.

Can you think of something that …
› you've managed to do to improve your health?
› should help students take their health more seriously?
› you're not prepared to try? (e.g., going on a diet)
› is unhealthy or dangerous and ought to be banned?
› the government needs to do to make people healthier?
› we're supposed to do to stay healthy (but you rarely do)?
› would be likely to encourage more people to get exercise?
› may prevent people from making unhealthy choices?

Personal Best   Write a short article about health myths in your country. Use different modal verbs and modal-like forms.   13

2 SKILLS LISTENING attitude and opinion ■ the disappearing /ə/ ■ life skills and well-being

2B My quest for quiet time

1 When you want some "quiet time," what activities do you do? What other activities do people do to relieve stress and improve their mental well-being?

2 ▶ 2.6 Watch or listen to the first part of *Talking Zone*. Which activity does each person below do to relieve stress?

3 A Complete the extracts with the correct form of the verbs in the box.

> collaborate   handle   cope   manage

1 I wasn't _____ my time properly. I was working too many hours and trying to fit too much in.
2 We all work on projects together. I just love _____ like that.
3 If I'm stressed or generally not _____ well with life's everyday problems, I do origami.
4 I tried meditating, but I just couldn't _____ the silence!

Go to Vocabulary practice: life skills and well-being, page 117

B Answer the questions in pairs.
1 How well do you manage your time when studying or at work?
2 Have you set any goals for yourself recently?
3 How do you cope with stress? What activities do you do to relieve stress?

Skill   understanding attitude and opinion

Understanding someone's attitude toward, or opinion of, something can be just as important as understanding factual content. Listen for:
- directly stated opinions, e.g., *I found it unbearable; If you ask me, yoga's the best therapy.*
- indirectly stated or "softened" opinions, e.g., *I'm not the biggest fan of mindfulness; I'm sure some people love art.*
- general attitude – does the speaker look and sound positive or negative about the topic?

Be careful. Speakers may first introduce an attitude or opinion that others hold, and then express a different personal opinion.

4 A ▶ 2.6 Read the Skill box. Watch or listen again. Are the sentences true (T) or false (F)?

1 Gemma believes that we're too busy nowadays.
2 She has a positive attitude toward experts who say we can manage anything if we set goals and persevere.
3 She considers herself to be a relaxed person.
4 She's found that going to the gym is a great way to relieve stress.
5 She had a negative experience with meditation.
6 Her attitude toward coloring books is extremely positive.

B Do you have similar opinions and attitudes to those expressed by Gemma?

attitude and opinion ■ the disappearing /ə/ ■ life skills and well-being   LISTENING   SKILLS   2B

5 ▶ 2.8 Watch or listen to the second part of the show and answer the questions.
1 What kind of therapy did a friend suggest that Gemma try?
2 Is this type of therapy new? In which situation was it first used?
3 Is Eric's attitude to this type of therapy positive or negative by the end of the show?

6 A ▶ 2.8 Watch or listen again. Complete the notes about Gemma's experience with one word in each blank.

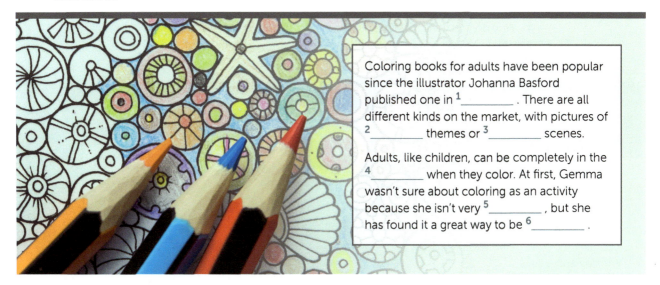

Coloring books for adults have been popular since the illustrator Johanna Basford published one in ¹_____ . There are all different kinds on the market, with pictures of ²_____ themes or ³_____ scenes.

Adults, like children, can be completely in the ⁴_____ when they color. At first, Gemma wasn't sure about coloring as an activity because she isn't very ⁵_____ , but she has found it a great way to be ⁶_____ .

B Did you use to enjoy coloring as a child? Would you like to do it now? Discuss your answers in pairs.

Listening builder — the disappearing /ə/ in fast speech

In fast speech, the /ə/ sound can disappear from the middle of some words. It usually disappears before the sounds /l/, /n/, and /r/ in longer words.
- before /l/: /trævələr/ (traveler) becomes /trævlər/
- before /n/: /pərsənəl/ (personal) becomes /pərsnəl/
- before /r/: /dʒenərəli/ (generally) becomes /dʒenrəli/

Sometimes the whole syllable disappears when the two consonants on either side of the /ə/ sound are the same.
- /laɪbrəri/ (library) becomes /laɪbri/ and /prɑbəbli/ (probably) becomes /prɑbli/.

7 A ▶ 2.9 Read the Listening builder. Look at the phrases in **bold** in the sentences below and underline the /ə/ sounds.
1 After trying **so many different things**, I wanted to do something that was, well, a little fun.
2 Art therapy was mainly a medical term as it was used for **patients recovering** from traumatic operations.
3 While today's art therapy is **definitely similar** in that people are using it to cope with stress, it's no longer just a medical thing.
4 I think this is **particularly interesting** because coloring books have become one of the most popular forms of mindful meditation.
5 And the next time you're in a café, **a library**, or even on a train, take a look around. **You'll probably** see somebody coloring.
6 Of course, **traditionally**, coloring was a children's activity.

B ▶ 2.9 Listen again and repeat. Practice saying the sentences quickly.

8 Discuss the questions in pairs.
1 In the show, Gemma says, "It's OK to slow down." To what extent do you need to slow down and take some more time for yourself?
2 Imagine doing a creative activity like drawing, coloring, or dancing. Would you prefer to do it on your own or in collaboration with others? Why?
3 Would you be interested in mindfulness activities as a way to relieve stress? Why/Why not?

Personal Best — Imagine that you own a well-being center. Write a paragraph describing the place and what people can do there.

2 LANGUAGE
modal verbs (2): advanced forms ■ verbs and nouns with the same form

2C Missing out?

1 Look at the two pictures in the text below. What are these people enjoying about their Saturday nights? Which activity do you generally prefer to do on the weekend?

2 Read the text. Then discuss the questions in pairs.
1 Why do you think FOMO is such a big problem today?
2 How often do you suffer from FOMO? Have you ever experienced JOMO?

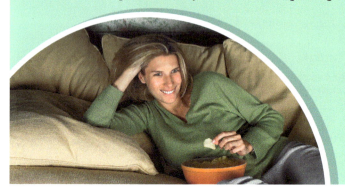

Bye-bye, FOMO. Hello, JOMO!

Are you ever concerned that your friends might be having way more fun than you? Do you check social media compulsively when you should be relaxing – or working – instead? Are you green with envy when scrolling through your friends' posts about their seemingly perfect and exciting social lives?

One survey has suggested that 56% of social media users suffer from FOMO (Fear of Missing Out) – a syndrome that's having a worrying impact on our generation. According to a colleague of mine, Liz, a self-confessed FOMO sufferer, "I see friends online apparently having the best time ever. I get that uneasy and all-consuming feeling that I'm missing out, and that my life, in comparison, is dull. I'm full of regrets about events I should have gone to, but didn't. My concerns about missing out mean that I often do way too much, and I'm burned out."

Luckily, the backlash has begun. Today's trendsetters are urging us to "reclaim our lives" and embrace JOMO (Joy of Missing Out) instead. JOMO means keeping your focus on doing what *you* want and selecting social commitments carefully. It means treating social media posts with healthy suspicion (your friends might not have been having as much fun as they appear in that photo!) and realizing that missing the "party of the year" isn't a sacrifice at all, because you'd much rather meet an old friend for dinner or simply watch bad comedies in your pajamas. JOMO followers did whatever they wanted last night. They didn't waste their whole evening wondering what they could have been doing, instead.

This season, JOMO is the new FOMO. For once, this is a trend with great benefits for everyone – it will make you healthier, happier, *and* save you money! Could the age of burnout be … well, burned out?

3 Underline sentences in the text that have the same meaning as sentences 1–5 below. Circle one verb in each sentence that has a noun form in the text.
1 FOMO is impacting our generation in a worrying way.
2 Liz regrets missing events she feels she should have gone to.
3 She often does too much because she's concerned about missing out.
4 JOMO lets you focus on doing things you want to do.
5 We can all greatly benefit from the trend for JOMO.

Go to Vocabulary practice: verbs and nouns with the same form, page 117

4 A Choose the correct auxiliary verbs to complete the sentences. Then check your answers in the text.
1 Do you check social media compulsively when you should *be / have* relaxing?
2 I'm full of regrets about events I should *be / have* gone to, but didn't.
3 Your friends might not *have / had* been having as much fun as they appear.

B Match sentences 1–3 in exercise 4A with forms a–c below. Then read the Grammar box.

a perfect ____ b continuous ____ c perfect continuous ____

modal verbs (2): advanced forms ■ verbs and nouns with the same form   LANGUAGE   2C

Grammar — modal verbs (2): advanced forms

Continuous:
I'm exhausted – I **must be doing** too much.
Paul looks fed up. He **might not be enjoying** himself.
You **shouldn't be working** – you're sick!

Perfect:
I **could have left** earlier last night.
You **shouldn't have gone** out if you didn't want to.
I **needn't have worried** about the test. It was easy.

Perfect continuous:
I **should have been working**, but I went out, instead.
Anna left early – she **can't have been feeling** well.
He **may have been driving** when you called.

Look! The perfect auxiliary verb *have* is always in the infinitive form:
She shouldn't **have** worried. NOT She shouldn't has worried.

Go to Grammar practice: modal verbs (2): advanced forms, page 97

5 A ▶ 2.13 **Pronunciation:** stress patterns with modal verb forms   Listen to the sentences. Which words in the verb phrases in **bold** have the most stress?

1 I **should have stayed** in last night after all.
2 That music's loud – our neighbors **must be having** a party!
3 Something amazing **might have been happening** while I was stuck at home.
4 I **ought to be studying** for my final exams.
5 He **couldn't have written** the address down correctly.
6 They **may not have been expecting** so many people to come.

B ▶ 2.13 Listen again and repeat.

6 A ▶ 2.14 Listen to three people talking about their attempts to reduce stress in their lives. Check (✓) the correct boxes.

	Speaker 1	Speaker 2	Speaker 3
Which speaker:			
1 finds it helpful to discuss problems?	☐	☐	☐
2 became sick gradually?	☐	☐	☐
3 learned a new skill to help him/her relax?	☐	☐	☐
4 became sick suddenly?	☐	☐	☐
5 received a present that helped him/her?	☐	☐	☐
6 doesn't get stressed easily?	☐	☐	☐

B ▶ 2.14 Complete the sentences with the correct form of the verbs in parentheses. Listen again and check.

1 Collapsing like that was pretty scary. It made me realize that I _____ too much. (must/do)
2 I knew that my boss _____ me so much work. (should/not/give)
3 I'd been getting splitting headaches, and I thought, "My body _____ to tell me something." (must/try)
4 I _____ about fitting in, though – everyone was friendly. (need/not/worry)
5 If I think I _____ too anxious about something, I just call up my friends. (might/get)
6 My friend Rob _____ when he said I was "as chilled out as a polar bear." (might/not/joke)

Go to Communication practice: Student A page 132, Student B page 143

7 In pairs, take turns telling your partner about something that:

- made you anxious, but that you needn't have worried about.
- you ought to have been doing this week, but haven't started yet.
- you shouldn't have said or that you shouldn't have done.
- you could be missing out on right now.
- you could have done if you hadn't gone out last weekend.
- your family or friends might be expecting you to do in the future.

Personal Best Write a paragraph about a time you "missed out" on something. Use different modal forms.

2 SKILLS WRITING giving constructive criticism ■ uses of *quite*

2D Highly recommended

1 In pairs, discuss the questions.
1 Do you use online review sites to find restaurants, activities, or courses? Which ones have you used?
2 What should a good review include in order to be useful?

2 A Quickly read a review about a climbing course. Which ratings do you think the reviewer, Jen, gave for each area below? Match areas 1–4 with ratings a–d.

1	Overall satisfaction	a	●●●●○	4/5
2	Price	b	●●●○○	3/5
3	Staff	c	●●○○○	2/5
4	Facilities	d	○○○○○	0/5

findacourse.com

Indoor Climbing Intro Course   Reviewed by Jen April 2 2018

I'd been wanting to try climbing for a while, and the day-long "Indoor Climbing Intro Course" at the White Rocks Center seemed ideal. It's described on the center's website as "highly recommended by *Climber's World* magazine," which sounded reassuring! Unfortunately, the course didn't quite live up to my expectations.

When I arrived, I was surprised to be placed in a large group of eighteen beginners. Although the course instructors, Tess and Ali, were extremely positive and encouraging, and they coped with the large number of participants quite well, in such a big class, it was difficult for them to give us much individual attention (this wasn't their fault, though). Most course participants climb rather slowly, and I feel we would have progressed more in a smaller group.

I also had one or two problems understanding what I was supposed to do, at times, as it was quite noisy, and I couldn't always hear the instructions. The facilities at the center are good, and, as a result, it seems to attract a lot of customers on weekends. Maybe it would be better to hold the course in a quieter area of the center, or on less busy days?

By the end of the day, I felt as though I'd only made slow progress, and I still hadn't managed to reach the top of the wall. Despite the fact that the course has excellent reviews, I found it fairly pricey, and, in my view, it wasn't economical at all. Overall, I'd say that the course might appeal to someone who already has a little experience climbing and is reasonably confident with heights. However, if you're genuinely a total beginner, like me, I'd suggest that you ask if the center could offer an introductory course, with fewer participants, on a quieter day. That would make quite a difference in the quality of the course.

B Do you think the review is helpful for the course organizers and for other readers? Why/Why not?

3 Read the review again and answer the questions.
1 What positive and negative points does Jen highlight?
2 When Jen highlights a negative point, does her language sound polite or rude?
3 What suggestions does Jen make?

Skill giving constructive criticism

When giving negative feedback, aim to keep any criticism constructive so that it is helpful.
• Aim for a sense of balance. Avoid highlighting only negative points – include positive ones, as well.
• Base your opinions on facts, and explain why your experience was positive or negative.
• Avoid generalizations (*Everything was awful.*) and more extreme or insulting language (*What a waste of time! The facilities were horrible!*).
• Make helpful suggestions and recommendations for improving the areas you are criticizing.

giving constructive criticism ■ uses of *quite* WRITING **SKILLS** **2D**

4 Read the Skill box. Then look at the following extracts from some reviews about a climbing course. Do they contain constructive criticism? If not, say how the writers could improve their reviews.

1 I'm sure the climbing wall was unsafe, although the instructors assured me that they were following the correct safety procedures. I just had a bad feeling about the place. I wouldn't recommend it at all.
2 Avoid this course! The center is difficult to find, there were too many people taking the course, the instructor didn't answer my questions completely, and also the drink machine was broken!
3 I joined the "improvers" class, but some of my classmates were complete beginners, and the pace was very slow. I think the center should encourage beginners to stick to the "beginners" class!

5 A Find four examples of *quite* in the review. What type of word does *quite* modify in each case? How does it change the meaning of these words?

> **Text builder** — uses of *quite*
>
> We use the adverb *quite* with adjectives, adverbs, verbs, and nouns. It can mean "pretty" or "fairly" with adjectives of degree.
> I was **quite** tired, but I continued climbing. (= pretty tired)
> I was **quite** confident I would do well. (= pretty confident)
> She learned **quite** quickly. (= pretty quickly)
> I'd heard the course was wonderful. **Quite** a disappointment! (= the complete opposite)
>
> **Look!** We use *not quite* to mean *not completely/exactly*. We can also use it to soften bad news or a negative opinion.
> I wasn't **quite** prepared for such a long class. I don't **quite** agree that it's the best course around.

B Read the Text builder and check your answers to exercise 5A.

6 Rewrite the sentences using *quite*.

1 The materials the teacher used were pretty helpful.
2 The whole place was a complete mess.
3 It's pretty difficult, but you'll improve with practice.
4 I didn't understand exactly how to use the equipment.
5 We all progressed reasonably quickly.
6 The website said the class was easy, so I wasn't completely ready for the actual difficulty.

7 A PREPARE Choose a course you have taken, or one of the courses below. Make notes about your positive and negative opinions of the course, based on the ratings categories in exercise 2A.

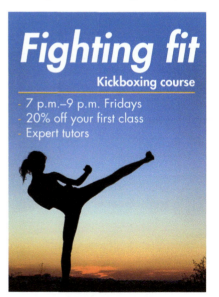

Fighting fit
Kickboxing course
- 7 p.m.–9 p.m. Fridays
- 20% off your first class
- Expert tutors

Love every moment
Mindfulness course
Takes place in the Main Hall at the Community Center, 10–11 a.m. every weekday. We provide mats.

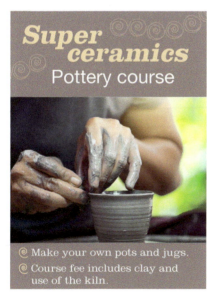

Super ceramics
Pottery course
@ Make your own pots and jugs.
@ Course fee includes clay and use of the kiln.

B PRACTICE Use the Skill box to help you write a review of the course. Include different uses of *quite*.

C PERSONAL BEST Work in groups. Exchange your reviews. Which review do you find most helpful? Why?

Personal Best Think of a product or service that you weren't totally satisfied with. Write a short review of it for a review site.

1 and 2 · REVIEW and PRACTICE

Grammar

1 Choose the correct options to complete the sentences.

1 *I've finished / I'm finishing* a 300-word essay, and now I'm watching TV to relax a little.

2 *I've been reading / I've read* the book *War and Peace*, but I don't remember many of the details.

3 My neighbors are driving me crazy. *It's / They're* the children that make all the noise.

4 Joe *should / manages to* be here any minute now. I've just checked his flight.

5 The company is formal. You *ought to / 're not supposed to* wear a suit.

6 You *needn't / must not* have worried about bringing dessert. I've got cake and ice cream.

7 Jenny *might be taking / might have been taking* a bath when you called. Try calling her again.

8 The tragedy *could have been / must have been* prevented. It's so sad.

9 *It / What* was most surprising was the fact that my brother had cooked!

10 Mom's *prepared / not prepared* to do our ironing any more. We have to do it ourselves.

2 Use the words in parentheses to complete the sentences so they mean the same as the first sentence.

1 Asil never remembers to close the door!
Asil _____ open! (leaving)

2 I like the way my boss, David, treats us.
What _____ the way he treats us. (about)

3 Sue texted me to invite me to dinner.
The _____ invite me to dinner. (reason)

4 I really think you should see a doctor immediately.
You _____ a doctor immediately. (better)

5 How long do you think the meeting will last?
How long is _____ last? (likely)

6 Working hard will not be a problem for Tim.
Tim _____ hard. (prepared)

7 I don't like the fact that Georgia wasn't wearing a seat belt!
Georgia _____ a seat belt! (should)

8 Paul bought lots of food unnecessarily.
Paul _____ so much food. (needn't)

9 I wasn't able to finish all the exam questions.
I _____ all the exam questions. (manage to)

10 Kay went abroad in 2011, 2016, and 2018.
Kay _____ three times. (been)

3 Choose the correct options to complete the text.

Four common mistakes we [1]*might be making / ought to be making* on the road to happiness

1 *Life events may not be that important*
People, in general, [2]*tend / are tending* not to think about the emotional impact of positive life events. Sure, you'll probably feel happier for a while if you buy a new car, or if you finally get the job you [3]*are dreaming / 've been dreaming* of for years. But we [4]*might not / shouldn't* forget that people usually get used to new circumstances, good and bad, which means that the enthusiasm [5]*is likely to / is supposed to* wear off after a couple of weeks.

2 *Trying to find out if we're really happy*
When we search for happiness, we obviously try to experience more joy and contentment. But to figure out if we [6]*make / are making* progress, we often compare how happy we feel at the moment to how happy we used to be. This creates a problem since, in the long run, [7]*what matter / what matters* most is experiencing happiness, not analyzing or studying it.

3 *Looking for happiness alone*
Happiness is mostly an individual state, so it's no surprise that when we look for happiness, we usually focus on ourselves. But a number of studies have shown that this [8]*could prevent / could have prevented* happiness and actually be a major source of depression. In other words, [9]*it's / they're* other people that can help us feel genuinely happy.

4 *Seeking intense experiences*
To be happy, we often look for strong emotions, like enthusiasm and excitement. But it [10]*doesn't need / needn't* to be like this. Research shows that happiness is caused by the frequency, rather than the intensity, of experiences we [11]*'ve had / 've been having*. If we focus on intensity, we end up setting goals that [12]*might / should* never be met.

Vocabulary

1 Circle the word that is different. Explain your answer.

1 sensitivity reliability fairness selfishness

2 annoyance generosity tolerance sacrifice

3 down to earth courageous conscientious disgusted

4 spine kidneys liver cast

5 sprain prioritize handle persevere

6 upset stomach splitting headache blister scan

REVIEW and PRACTICE 1 and 2

2 Complete the sentences with the correct form of the verbs in the box.

> benefit   have (x2)   pick up   prioritize   pull
> set   take (x2)

1 Leo fell down the stairs and _____ a dozen or so stitches on his forehead.
2 Don't come too near me – I think I must have _____ a bug somewhere.
3 Should antibiotics be _____ before or after meals?
4 My voice is a little weird because I've just _____ an injection in my mouth.
5 _____ a muscle is something that happens to everyone, but the degree of pain varies from person to person.
6 Thousands of households have _____ greatly from the new policies.
7 My manager told me I should learn how to _____ my workload and _____ goals at the beginning of every week. She also said, "If you notice that something isn't working, _____ the initiative to try to fix it."

3 Complete the text with the correct form of the words in parentheses.

> **Do you have the ¹_____ (aware) you need to live a purposeful and fulfilling life?**
>
> Most specialists agree that people who *get carried away* with negative thoughts find it harder to *deal with* stress and are more likely to have health problems such as heart conditions and high blood pressure. Conventional ²_____ (wise) tells us that we should stay positive, be ³_____ (thank) for what we have, and try to *look on the bright side*. But are they right?
> In all ⁴_____ (honest), I think this is the wrong way to cope with life's ups and downs. Most people don't have much ⁵_____ (tolerate) for life's problems, and this is actually where the main problem lies. We need to accept that life will always bring difficulty, and that most painful emotions will naturally come and go. All we need is a little ⁶_____ (patient).
> So, if you're in a bad mood, don't automatically try to *cheer up*. Accept that you're *feeling down* and trust that the feeling will eventually pass.

4 Match the expressions in *italics* in exercise 3 with definitions a–e below.

a become (or make someone) happier when sad
b handle or respond successfully to a situation or feeling
c have an optimistic and positive approach to life
d be depressed or unhappy
e get excited or feel too much emotion

Personal Best

Lesson 1A
Write four sentences about your life using simple, continuous, or perfect aspects of the present.

Lesson 1A
Write three sentences about yourself that describe your attitudes and emotions.

Lesson 1B
Describe four past habits of people you know.

Lesson 1C
Describe three qualities you look for in a friend, beginning with *what*, *the thing*, or *the reason*.

Lesson 1C
Write three cleft sentences about things you feel strongly about.

Lesson 1D
Write a short dialogue where one person asks for clarification and the other rephrases the sentence.

Lesson 2A
Name six medical problems. Give advice or a recommendation for each.

Lesson 2A
Give three pieces of advice for a friend who's been working too hard.

Lesson 2B
Name three things you can do to increase your well-being.

Lesson 2C
Describe three things you could, should, or needn't have done last week.

Lesson 2C
Name five nouns and verbs that have the same form.

Lesson 2D
Write two sentences with *quite* and with *not quite.*

21

UNIT 3 Looking back

LANGUAGE past time ■ change and time

3A Sign of the times

1 Look at these objects from the late twentieth century. In pairs, discuss which items have:

1 changed significantly **in your lifetime**.
2 **become** (or are becoming) **obsolete**.
3 **gone out of fashion** (or **come back into fashion**).
4 **evolved** into something different.

Go to Vocabulary practice: change and time, page 118

2 In pairs, think of two objects that did not exist in the era when your grandparents were young. Do you think these objects will still exist in 50 years? How might they change?

3 A ▶ 3.3 Listen to David and Lena talking about three objects from the British Museum's collection "A History of the World in 100 Objects." Choose the correct options to complete the sentences.

A History of the World in 100 Objects

1 It's a stone belt used *to play the oldest ballgame in the world / only during special sports events*.
2 It's a stone which helped translate *Egyptian hieroglyphic symbols / Ancient Greek*.
3 It's one of the *first ever emojis / most popular images in the world*.

B What objects did David and Lena suggest to represent life today? What would you choose? Why?

4 ▶ 3.3 Listen to David and Lena's conversation again. Are the sentences true (T) or false (F)?

1 People in Mesoamerica **used to play** a game similar to baseball. ____
2 Players protected themselves with leather belts while they **were playing**. ____
3 They **would kick** the ball into the air. ____
4 Scholars **had been trying** to understand hieroglyphics long before the Rosetta Stone was found. ____
5 The stone **enabled** scholars to translate the hieroglyphs. ____
6 *The Great Wave* **had been used** on many different products before it became an emoji. ____

past time ■ change and time   **LANGUAGE 3A**

5 Match the forms in **bold** in exercise 4 with functions a–d below. Then read the Grammar box.
   a habitual actions or states in the past   ____ ____
   b single actions in the past   ____
   c continuous actions in the past   ____ ____
   d events that happened before the main event being described ____ ____

> **Grammar past time**
>
> **Past narration:**
> It **was raining** hard when they **found** the treasure.
> People **had been searching** for it for over a century.
> When they **opened** the box, they **discovered** that all the coins **had become** rusty.
>
> **Habitual past:**
> People **didn't use to have** access to healthcare.
> They **often went** without treatment.
> The farmers **would work** in the fields all day.
> They **were always telling** us to work harder.
>
> **Look!** We use different narrative tenses for specific times and functions, e.g., the past continuous to set the scene or to describe an action in progress in the past:
> That summer, we **were staying** in the country. When the storm struck, we **were having** lunch.
>
> However, habitual past forms have similar meanings. We vary them in order to avoid repetition:
> We **used to go** away every summer, and we **often ended up** near the ocean, where we**'d go** sailing.

Go to Grammar practice: past time, page 98

6 A ▶ 3.5 **Pronunciation:** weak forms of *had* and *been* Listen and notice how the speakers say *had* and *been* in the past perfect continuous.
   1 Tim and Jan **had been traveling** for hours.
   2 The shopkeeper thought Tom **had been stealing** from him.
   3 It looked as though the neighbors **had been decorating** their house.
   4 I didn't know that our sales manager **had been working** abroad.
   5 I told her that everyone **had been listening** to her conversation.
   6 It was obvious that Carl **had been practicing** his speech.

   B ▶ 3.5 Listen again and repeat.

7 A Choose the correct options to complete the text about an important object.

When I was younger, my friends [1]*had thought / used to think* I was really fortunate because my dad was obsessed with video games. At dawn every day, I [2]*heard / 'd hear* loud cheers from the living room as he squeezed in some gaming before breakfast. Every now and then, he [3]*'d get / 'd got* out some of the old games he [4]*was playing / 'd played* as a teenager, almost three decades earlier. Although they [5]*used to go / 'd gone* out of fashion, they were fun, but also pretty annoying as you had to switch consoles and plug in different equipment. Dad [6]*would often talk / had often been talking* about the idea of a games console you could play any game on. Then one day, while I [7]*had been / was* googling something else, I [8]*discovered / was discovering* that a company [9]*would make / had made* the console Dad had [10]*dreamed / been dreaming* of! The "Retrobox" has over 1,200 retro games on it, and I got my dad one. He felt like all his birthdays had come at once!

   B ▶ 3.6 Listen and check your answers.

   Go to Communication practice: Student A page 132, Student B page 143

8 Think of three important objects from your life or the life of someone in your family. Tell your partner about the history of the objects and the memories they hold.

Personal Best Write a paragraph about something that you wish hadn't become obsolete.   23

3 SKILLS

READING text structure and organization ■ narrating the future from the past

3B A remarkable life

1 Tell your partner about a remarkable person that you admire. Why, in your opinion, is he/she remarkable?

2 Quickly read the text on page 25. Who was Helen Keller? What was remarkable about her life?

3 Read the text again. Match headings 1–6 with paragraphs A–F.

1 Helping others   _____
2 An amazing discovery   _____
3 A difficult start   _____
4 Learning quickly   _____
5 Among the greats   _____
6 A legacy that lives on   _____

> **Skill**   **understanding text structure and organization**
>
> **Writers use different techniques for connecting and organizing ideas. Recognizing these can help you understand the text better.**
> - Notice how ideas are organized in a logical order, both within and across paragraphs.
> - Look for organizing words (e.g., *whereas*, *therefore*, *consequently*) that show relationships such as comparison, contrast, cause, effect, reason, purpose, and result.
> - Pay attention to pronouns (e.g., *it*, *his*, *those*), adverbs of time and place (e.g., *then*, *there*), or other words (e.g., *both*, *neither*, *all*) that refer to information in other sentences or paragraphs.
> - Look for key nouns or synonyms that are repeated, substitution words (e.g., *I had two* **solutions**. *The first* **one** *...*), and omitted words (e.g., *I looked for some milk. There wasn't any.*).

4 Read the Skill box. Then read the sentences below, which have been removed from the text. Match the sentences with the blanks in the text (1–5). There is one extra sentence you don't need.

a She would comment that she could always recognize him by the distinctive smell of his cigars.
b Sullivan used a radical method to teach Helen to recognize letters by spelling out words on the girl's hand.
c Sullivan quickly built a positive relationship with Helen, and the young girl made rapid progress.
d In desperation, her parents sought contact with anyone who had experience with their daughter's disabilities.
e She immediately realized the significance of this; if water had a name, then so did everything else.
f Consequently, Helen was unable to go through with her plans and remained single forever.

5 Read paragraph A again. Underline the phrase that refers to Helen's future.

> **Text builder**   **narrating the future from the past**
>
> In texts such as biographies and novels, the narrative is usually in the past. However, writers can refer to a future event from the point of view of the past narrative.
> *was/were* + infinitive: *They **were to become** influential in their field.*
> *would* + *go on* + infinitive: *The young scientist **would go on to make** important discoveries.*
> *would later* + base form: *The young man **would later grow up** to be president.*
> *be destined* + infinitive: *She **was destined to become** an award-winning writer.*

6 Read the Text builder. Then find one example of each structure in paragraphs B, C, and D.

7 In pairs, discuss the questions.

1 What do you think Helen Keller's most amazing achievement was?
2 If you were interviewing Helen, what questions would you ask her?

text structure and organization ■ narrating the future from the past   READING   SKILLS   3B

OUT OF THE
darkness

A   When *Time* magazine nominated their most influential people of the last century, it included Albert Einstein, Nelson Mandela, and Mahatma Gandhi. It also included a remarkable person who spent most of her life both deaf and blind, but who would go on to play an important part in many of the significant social and cultural movements of the twentieth century.

B   Helen Keller was born into a middle-class family in the state of Alabama in 1880. Helen was an unusually precocious child; she was walking and talking to her parents by the age of one. However, tragedy soon struck when, at the age of 19 months, Helen was afflicted by an unknown illness that left her both deaf and blind. As Helen grew older, she developed a simple sign language with a companion, but her frustration at not being able to communicate in more depth manifested itself through violent mood swings. ¹_____ . Their efforts led them to the inventor of the telephone, Alexander Bell, who was working with deaf children. Bell directed them to the Perkins Institution for the Blind in Boston, and it was a recent graduate of the institution, Anne Sullivan, who was to become the most instrumental person in Helen's extraordinary journey. The Kellers invited her to come and live with them as Helen's tutor. Little did they know that Helen and Anne would go on to become lifelong friends.

C   ²_____ . The early results of this were unpromising. Helen either refused to cooperate or was unable to understand what Sullivan was trying to communicate to her. However, Sullivan persisted, and the breakthrough came one day when she placed Helen's hand under a stream of cold water, spelling the letters W-A-T-E-R on Helen's other hand. At last, Helen understood. She would later explain that she suddenly realized that the wonderful cool substance flowing over her hand had a name, and it was represented by the shapes made by her tutor's hand. ³_____ . Helen indicated more objects to Sullivan, wanting to know how to spell them, and by the end of the day, she had learned 30 words.

D   Over the following years, Helen's thirst for learning was insatiable. She attended speech classes at schools for the deaf; she also studied regular school subjects like English, where her talent for writing was noticed; she became proficient in new methods of communication, including touch-lip reading, Braille, and typing. Learning to speak took many more years of hard work, but eventually she succeeded at that, too. The story of Helen's remarkable achievements was spreading across the country, and she met a number of famous people, including the writer Mark Twain, with whom she became good friends. ⁴_____ . Eventually, Helen was accepted at Radcliffe College, the sister institution of the then all-male Harvard College. In 1904, she became the first deaf-blind person in the U.S. to earn a college degree, and it was generally accepted that she was destined to achieve great things in her life.

E   Helen devoted her career to campaigning to improve the lives of deaf and blind people throughout the world, as well as being an advocate for women's rights, workers' rights, and the peace movement. In 1915, she founded Helen Keller International, an institute which has helped combat some of the major causes of blindness in the world; today it continues to benefit millions of people. She traveled to 35 countries on five continents, meeting world leaders and thousands of deaf and blind people. By then Helen had a huge international profile and, in many countries, her visits attracted great numbers of people and helped draw attention to the challenges facing people with disabilities. Ironically, Helen was a victim of the prejudices that she was working so hard to eradicate. While in her late thirties, she fell in love and planned to marry, but her family – so supportive in every other way – objected, believing, like many at the time, that people with disabilities should not marry. ⁵_____ .

F   Helen died in 1968 at the age of 87. She was, and continues to be, an inspiration to millions for her incredible achievements in the face of adversity and her selfless desire to help others.

Helen (right) meets U.S. President John F. Kennedy

Personal Best   Write a paragraph about the early life of someone who would go on to achieve great things.

25

3 LANGUAGE
comparison ■ expressions with *come* and *go*

3C Delicious discoveries

1 In pairs, ask and answer the following questions.
1 Does cooking **come easily** to you?
2 **When it comes to** food, what's your guiltiest pleasure?
3 When you are choosing a meal, what **comes first**: flavor, nutritional value, or price?
4 Have you ever tried to cook something where everything **went wrong**?
5 What would you choose to **keep you going** until your next meal?

Go to Vocabulary practice: expressions with *come* and *go*, page 119

2 Look at the pictures of the items of food below. Which one do you think was discovered first? Read the text and check.

Delicious discoveries and how they've evolved

Many of today's most popular convenience foods have been around a lot longer than you might think. **Laura Green** takes us through a brief history of some of our favorites.
Many of us consider pizza the ultimate modern convenience food, but, actually, it's just as ancient as bison steaks, having been invented in the Stone Age! Cooked on hot rocks with meat toppings, the bases were significantly darker and heavier than modern ones, and they had a long way to ¹*come / go* before they became the cheesy treats we know today. It wasn't until the nineteenth century that bakers in Naples, Italy, made mozzarella, basil, and tomato pizzas to represent the colors of the Italian flag. Over the years, pizza toppings have become more and more inventive, but that simple Neapolitan pizza is still one of the most popular.

Amazingly, ice cream is almost as ancient as pizza, and the oldest recipe is by far the simplest. In the fifth century B.C., Greeks simply mixed snow with honey and fruit. The first modern recipes for ice cream appeared in the eighteenth century. Of course, cooks in those days ²*came / went* up against the problem of freezing the milk, so early ice cream was not nearly as firm as its modern-day equivalent. It ³*comes / goes* without saying that ice cream was an expensive luxury. U.S. President George Washington loved it so much, he spent $200 on ice cream in 1790 alone – the equivalent of almost $3,000 today!

Compared to pizza and ice cream, breakfast cereals are a relatively modern invention. In the nineteenth century, vegetarians created cereals as an alternative to the traditional cooked breakfast. Early cereals were marketed as being twice as healthy as meat and just as filling – a bowlful could keep you ⁴*coming / going* all morning. When it ⁵*comes / goes* to taste, though, these early cereals were far less appetizing than cereals today. The first granola was as hard as rock, while cornflakes were chewy rather than crunchy. Cereals were also nowhere near as sweet as many modern equivalents. Nowadays, a single bowl of cereal may contain far more sugar than a chocolate cookie – it seems that the more our food evolves, the less healthy it becomes!

3 A Read the text again. For items 1–5, choose the correct form of *come* or *go*.

B Does the earlier or the modern version of each food sound more appetizing? Why?

4 A Complete the comparative sentences below. Then check your answers in the text.
1 Pizza is _____ as ancient _____ bison steaks.
2 Prehistoric pizza bases were _____ darker and heavier _____ modern ones.
3 Over the years, pizza toppings have become _____ and _____ inventive.
4 Ice cream is almost _____ ancient _____ pizza.
5 Early ice cream was _____ firm _____ modern ice cream.
6 Cereals were _____ sweet _____ many modern equivalents.

26

comparison ■ expressions with *come* and *go*   LANGUAGE **3C**

B Match sentences 1–6 in exercise 4A with the types of comparison a–d. below. Then read the Grammar box.
a a big difference in a quality, an amount, etc. ___ ___ ___
b a small difference in a quality, an amount, etc. ___
c no difference in a quality, an amount, etc. ___
d a change over time of a quality, an amount, etc. ___

Grammar comparison

Modifying comparisons:
It's **not any** saltier **than** the other.
This soup is **slightly less** tasty.
It's **a good deal smaller than** it was.

Modifying as (... as) comparisons:
It works **just as** well **as** we'd hoped.
It's **not quite as** big **as** it used to be.
It's **nowhere near as** nice.

Double comparatives:
The harder he worked, **the more successful** the business became.
The more we ate, **the less** we talked.

Progressive comparatives:
Exams are getting **harder and harder**.
Our diet is becoming **less and less healthy**.
This train is moving **more and more slowly**.

Look! When modifying a comparison, be aware of how formal or informal the modifier is:
Thanks so much for replacing the faulty plug. It's **way** considerably safer than it was.

Go to Grammar practice: comparison, page 99

5 A ▶ 3.10 **Pronunciation:** /ə/ sound Listen and notice how the speakers say the vowel sounds in the parts in **bold**.
1 Frozen pizza is nowhere near **as** tasty **as** homemade pizza.
2 It's becoming hard**er and** hard**er** to find decent coffee.
3 Argentinian beef is far bett**er than** beef produced anywhere else.
4 Making bread is a good deal cheap**er than** buying it.
5 **The** more healthily we eat, **the** happi**er** we are.
6 People are becoming less **and** less able to cook well.

B ▶ 3.10 Listen again and repeat. Which of these statements do you agree with?

6 A ▶ 3.11 Listen to Luke and Marie discussing snacks. Which two snacks that they discuss are named after people? What are the stories behind them?

B ▶ 3.11 Listen again and choose the correct options to complete the sentences.
1 Luke thinks store-bought guacamole is *slightly less tasty than / nowhere near as tasty as* freshly-made guacamole.
2 Marie thinks that salsa from a jar is *far tastier than / just as good as* fresh salsa.
3 When Marie eats too much prepared food, she just feels *worse and worse / slightly worse*.
4 Luke says that the more prepared food you eat, *the more you want to eat / the better you feel*.
5 Luke thinks that sandwiches *are far better / aren't quite as good* at filling you up.
6 Marie doesn't find sandwiches *any less tempting than / as tempting as* nachos.

Go to Communication practice: Student A page 133, Student B page 144

7 In pairs, discuss the sentences below.

From strength to strength or a **long way to go?**

① Fifty years ago, children were significantly happier than they are nowadays.
② The problems that teens come up against in daily life are getting more and more challenging.
③ People today are nowhere near as open-minded or as tolerant as they were in the past.
④ When it comes to social media, the more it develops, the easier it will be to make good friends.
⑤ Life today isn't any more rewarding than it was 100 years ago.
⑥ In general, as a society we're going from strength to strength, but we still have a long way to go.

Personal Best Write a short paragraph comparing two food takeout or delivery services you have used.

27

3 SKILLS SPEAKING reminiscing ■ fixing errors

3D The time of my life

1 Think back to what your life was like at the three stages below. What are/were the best and worst things about each stage? Discuss your ideas in pairs.

- childhood
- teenage years
- college years

2 ▶ 3.12 Watch or listen to the first part of *Talking Zone* and answer the questions.

1 Which stage of life do Abigail and Ben think was the best time of their lives?
2 What do they think about each other's choices?

3 A Complete the sentences from the conversation with the words in the box.

> retrospect   hindsight   back   time   past   days   think

1 If I could turn back _____ , I'd go back in a second. Those were the _____ !
2 When I _____ back to that time, I just remember never having any money.
3 With the benefit of _____ , I should've worked harder.
4 The Del Funk Trio? Now that takes me _____ !
5 In _____ , a lot of my happiest memories come from that time.
6 The Tracey Clancy Show? What a blast from the _____ !

B ▶ 3.12 Match sentences 1–6 in exercise 3A with options a–e. Use one option twice. Watch or listen again and check your answers.

a Abigail talking about her childhood.   _____
b Ben talking about his college days.   _____
c Ben talking about a TV show.   _____
d Abigail talking about her college days.   _____
e Abigail talking about a concert.   _____

Conversation builder — reminiscing

Introductory phrases
When I look / think back, ...
When I think back to / look back on, ...
If I remember right, ...
It's all coming back to me now.

Exclamations
That takes me back!
What a blast from the past!
Those were the days!
Good/Fun/Crazy times!

The past from the present
In retrospect, ...
With the benefit of hindsight, ...
If I could turn back time, ...

4 In pairs, complete sentences 1–6. Discuss your memories.

1 When I think back to the first home we lived in, what I most remember is …
2 When I look back on my teens, the person I most looked up to was …
3 I remember that TV show! What a blast from the past! Wasn't it … ?
4 With the benefit of hindsight, I should have …
5 If I could turn back time, I would have chosen to … , instead of …
6 In retrospect, I think the best days of my life were … Those were the days!

28

reminiscing ■ fixing errors **SPEAKING** SKILLS **3D**

5 ▶ 3.13 Watch or listen to the second part of the show and answer the questions.
1 Which memory does Abigail talk about?
2 Who was she with at the time? What happened in the end?

6 ▶ 3.13 Complete the sentences with two words in each blank. Watch or listen again and check.
1 Anna … _____ Hannah! Is that right?
2 She decided that she'd always wanted to, _____ , that she'd always wanted to do a bungee jump.
3 It wasn't far and, well, I couldn't, _____ , I just wanted to be a good friend, I suppose.

Skill fixing errors

We all make errors in meaning, grammatical errors, and false starts. There are several different ways we can deal with these:
- If you make a false start, add, *you know*, and start again, e.g., *I've always wanted to, you know, I've always wanted to visit Turkey.*
- Or start again with a reformulated sentence, e.g., *I've always wanted to, you know, it's my dream to visit Turkey.*
- Fix an error you have made with *I mean*, e.g., *She's American, I mean, Australian.*

7 A Read the Skill box. Which sentences in exercise 6 are examples of each strategy for fixing errors?

B ▶ 3.14 Match 1–6 with a–f to make full sentences. Listen and check. Practice saying the sentences.
1 We've been trying to, you know,
2 I have to go now, but I'll see you tomorrow,
3 I've not been able to, you know,
4 Does your brother still fix dishwashers,
5 Gary is a nice guy, but he's a little,
6 Don't drive into town. There's a big, you know,

a I haven't contacted the bank yet, sorry.
b you know, we're not great friends.
c there's a big game. Traffic will be awful!
d I mean, later this evening.
e we've been trying to spend less money.
f I mean, washing machines?

Go to Communication practice: Students A and B page 133

8 A PREPARE Complete the question with an adjective from the box. Plan how you will answer it.
What's the _____ thing that happened to you during your high school or college days?

funniest   scariest   weirdest   most nail-biting   most heart-warming
most embarrassing   most disastrous   most coincidental

B PRACTICE Take turns telling your story using reminiscing expressions. Fix any errors you make.
C PERSONAL BEST Give your partner feedback on his/her story. Did he/she use reminiscing expressions and fix any errors? Choose a different adjective and take turns telling another story.

Personal Best Write a short conversation between you and a friend reminiscing about the first time you met.

UNIT 4
Success and failure

LANGUAGE verb patterns (1): infinitives and *-ing* forms ■ success and failure

4A Brilliant failure

1 A What do you know about the success stories of the people in the pictures? Apart from being successful, what else do you think they might have in common?

B ▶ 4.1 Listen to an interview with Dr. Arends, an expert on success and failure. What do the four people in the pictures all have in common?

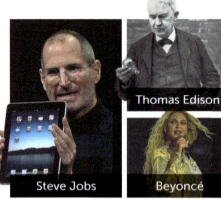

Steve Jobs Thomas Edison Beyoncé Michael Jordan

2 Complete the ideas from the interview with the words in the box.

> lead triumph fulfill expectations back success

1 Michael Jordan didn't let his failure to get on the school basketball team hold him _____ . In fact, it motivated him to work even harder to _____ his dream.
2 Beyoncé's first band wasn't the _____ story in the news, but it made her more determined, and, in the end, she was able to _____ over failure to become one of the most successful performers ever.
3 When Apple launched its first electronic notepad, it went over like a _____ balloon. However, the iPad, which was based on the same technology, later exceeded everyone's _____ .

Go to Vocabulary practice: success and failure, page 120

3 ▶ 4.1 Complete the advice with the correct form of the verbs in parentheses. Listen again and check.

Failing miserably can **help us thrive!**

- Embrace failure. We can learn from our mistakes – but it's no good ¹_____ them! (ignore)
- Failure can make us stronger if we don't let it ²_____ us back. (hold)
- Failure can also encourage us ³_____ creative. (be)
- Mistakes can give us something ⁴_____ about. (think)

- If you can imagine yourself ⁵_____ something, you should go for it! (do)
- Remember that many of the most successful people ever ⁶_____ were also amazing failures. (exist)
- If you mess something up, you should do anything except ⁷_____ up! (give)
- There are plenty of ways ⁸_____ failure into success! (turn)

4 Match the sentences in exercise 3 with rules a–h below. Then read the Grammar box.

- We use the infinitive:
  a after verbs such as *advise, encourage, tell,* and *warn* + object. ____
  b after words such as *enough, plenty of* + noun, or *too* + adjective. ____
  c after superlative adjectives + noun. ____
  d after words like *something, anywhere,* and *nowhere*. ____
- We use the base form:
  e after the verbs *let, make,* and *help* + object. ____
  f after words like *except, but,* and *than*. ____
- We use the *-ing* form:
  g after phrases such as *there's no point, it's no good,* and *it's no use*. ____
  h after verbs such as *imagine, dislike, keep,* and *mind* + object. ____

30

verb patterns (1): infinitives and -ing forms ■ success and failure   LANGUAGE 4A

Grammar — verb patterns (1): infinitives and -ing forms

We use infinitives after
- some verbs + object:
  She **told** me **not to look**.
- *something*, *anywhere*, etc.:
  It gave me **something to focus** on.
- superlatives and *the first*, *the next*, etc.:
  She's **the youngest** person **to win**.
  He was **the first** person **to climb** Everest.
- quantifiers:
  We didn't have **enough** time **to finish** it.
  I have **too much** work **to do**.

We use the base form and not the infinitive after
- *let*, *make*, and *help* + object:
  They **helped me see** things differently.
- object + *and*, *or*, *but*, *except*, and *than*:
  He does nothing **but watch** TV all day.

We use -ing forms after
- some verbs (+ object):
  She always **keeps him waiting**.
- expressions with *It* ... and *There's no* ...:
  There's no point deceiving yourself.

Look! We can also use perfect infinitives and -ing forms to talk about a completed or past action.
She was the first **to try** it./She was the first **to have tried** it.
I regret **telling** her your secret./I regret **having told** her your secret.

Go to Grammar practice: verb patterns (1): infinitives and -ing forms, page 100

5 A ▶ 4.5 **Pronunciation:** linking after *to* Listen to the sentences. Is there a sound you don't hear after *to*? Circle Y (yes) or N (no).
1 Support from his family helped him **to** accomplish a great deal.   Y / N
2 She was too determined **to** give up that easily.   Y / N
3 They didn't expect us **to** ask so many questions.   Y / N
4 They were delighted **to** have passed with flying colors.   Y / N
5 Hard work is the best way **to** meet your targets.   Y / N
6 I advised her **to** apologize for the error.   Y / N

B ▶ 4.5 When is a sound not pronounced after *to*? Listen again and repeat.

6 A Complete the sentences with the correct form of the verbs in parentheses.
1 You should never make children _____ anything they don't want to do. (do)
2 The best way _____ someone _____ harder is to criticize them. (encourage, work)
3 Most people aren't brave enough _____ their dreams. (follow)
4 You should do anything except _____ the law to achieve what you want in life. (break)
5 There's no point _____ to become famous if you're not talented. (attempt)
6 We all dislike other people _____ more successful than we are. (be)

B In pairs, discuss whether you agree or disagree with the statements in exercise 6A.

Go to Communication practice: Student A page 134, Student B page 144

7 Are you and your friends motivators? Do you tend to encourage or discourage each other? Take the questionnaire and discuss your answers in pairs.

Friends: cheer them on or hold them back?

1 Can you think of a time when a friend helped you fulfill a goal?
2 Have you ever done anything to help a friend who was about to miss a deadline?
3 Are most of your friends too busy to take much of an interest in your dreams?
4 Have you ever encouraged a friend when he/she was lacking in confidence?
5 Do you remember ever having told a friend he/she was to blame for something?
6 "Following your dreams is a waste of time." Have you ever said this?

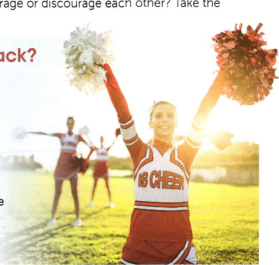

Personal Best Write some advice for your best friend, using *There's no point ...* , *Don't let anyone ...* , *Don't expect other people ...*

31

4 SKILLS LISTENING reasons and outcomes ■ linking ■ expressions with *make* and *take*

4B Make more mistakes!

1 A Read the sentences about mistakes. What do the phrases in **bold** mean?
1. When I make a mistake, I always **take it** pretty **badly**. I'm hard on myself, I guess I'm a bit of a perfectionist.
2. If I make a mistake that affects other people, I always apologize and try to **make it up** to them by doing something nice or helpful.
3. When something goes wrong, I always try to **make the best** of a bad situation and learn from my mistakes.

B Are the sentences in exercise 1A true for you? Discuss your ideas in pairs.

Go to Vocabulary practice: expressions with *make* and *take*, page 120

2 **4.7** Watch or listen to the first part of *Talking Zone*. Answer the questions below.
1. What is Taylor's vlog called?
2. How did Taylor first get the idea to start the vlog?
3. Which mistake does Taylor talk about?
4. What does Taylor say the message of his vlog is?

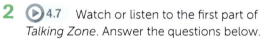

Skill understanding reasons and outcomes

People often talk about reasons for, and outcomes of, a situation. Try to understand how these ideas are linked.
- Listen for words or phrases that express reasons and outcomes, e.g., *as, since, due to, because of, on account of, so/such ... that, consequently, as a result, ... (it) resulted in ... , (it) led to ... , ... this meant that ...*
- Listen for the use of different tenses. The reason is usually further back in the past than the outcome, although either could be stated first in a sentence, e.g., *The man got really angry because I'd driven into his wall. I'd driven into the man's wall, so he got really angry.*
- Listen for the use of the third conditional, which gives a hypothetical outcome, e.g., *If she hadn't gone to the party, she wouldn't have met him.* (= She went, and she did meet him.)

3 **4.7** Read the Skill box. Watch or listen again and choose the correct option to answer the questions.

1. What was the outcome of Rich's mistake?
   a. He upset his boss.
   b. He met his girlfriend.
   c. He got a new job.

2. What was the outcome of Sara's mistake?
   a. Her colleagues took it badly and were upset.
   b. She never saw her mug again.
   c. She had to tell the whole office she'd got it wrong.

3. Why were Cathy's classmates laughing?
   a. She was embarrassed.
   b. She'd looked up the wrong word.
   c. She'd used the wrong word.

4. What was the main reason people liked "The Passenger Seat"?
   a. They found it hilarious.
   b. They loved the outcome of Taylor's mistake.
   c. They liked Taylor's message to "make more mistakes."

reasons and outcomes ■ linking ■ expressions with *make* and *take* **LISTENING** **SKILLS** **4B**

4 Imagine you want to post a story about a mistake on Taylor's vlog. What story would you post? Tell your partner.

5 ▶ 4.8 Watch or listen to the second part of the show. Complete the sentences with one word in each blank.
 1 The second video on Taylor's vlog is about mistakes with _____ outcomes.
 2 Taylor had always taken it for _____ that mistakes were a bad thing.
 3 "Poka yoke" means the _____ of mistakes.
 4 At the end, Taylor says that we should all _____ time to _____ more mistakes.

6 A ▶ 4.8 Watch or listen again. Answer the questions.
 1 What mistake did Harley Windsor's mother make?
 2 What were the outcomes of her mistake?
 3 What did Raheen Bhakta do by mistake?
 4 What happened as a result of his mistake?
 5 What do the three pictures on the right have in common?

B What other examples of poka yoke can you think of in cars and electrical appliances? Can you think of any that you would like to see in other products?

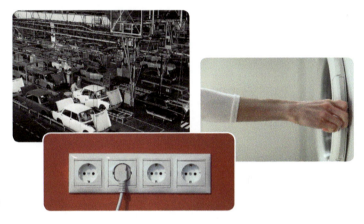

Listening builder | **linking consonants and vowels**

We usually connect words together in continuous speech by linking the sound at the end of one word to the sound at the beginning of the next word.
- Consonant sounds often link to other consonant and vowel sounds:
  It's‿no joke. (sounds like *It snow joke*.) My‿seat (sounds like *mice eat*)
- Similar consonant sounds link together and are pronounced only once:
  I'd‿drive‿Fred‿to the station but my car's‿stuck in the mud.
- Vowel sounds can be linked to other vowel sounds by adding /w/ or /y/:
  - We add a /w/ when a word ends in /uː/, /əʊ/, or /aʊ/:
    You‿aren't late.   No,‿I can't.   How‿are you?
    /w/   /w/   /w/
  - We add a /y/ when a word ends in /iː/, /aɪ/, or /eɪ/:
    The‿end.   I‿asked him.   May‿I sit here?
    /y/   /y/   /y/

7 A Read the Listening builder. Look at extracts 1–6 and mark where the links are. Add /w/ or /y/ where necessary.
 1 Hello everyone.
 2 I'd do it again.
 3 Mistakes often have positive outcomes.
 4 So I decided to make a video about it.
 5 They found themselves outside an ice-skating rink.
 6 He agreed to help pay her course fees.

B ▶ 4.9 Listen and check. Then practice saying the sentences.

8 In pairs, discuss the questions below.
 1 What was the last mistake you made? What happened?
 2 Have you made any mistakes that have had positive outcomes? What were they?
 3 Which of the stories about mistakes from this lesson do you find the most memorable? Why?

Personal Best Write a paragraph about a mistake you or somebody else made. Give the reason for the mistake and its outcomes.

4 LANGUAGE — adding emphasis (2): inversion and *do/does/did* ■ idioms

4C Making it big

1 In pairs, discuss the questions.
1 Do you follow any YouTube channels or blogs? If so, which ones? If not, why not?
2 What, in your opinion, makes a good video channel or blog?

2 A Read the text about two successful YouTube stars. What are their videos about? What motivated them to start posting videos?

Making it **big** online
Sometimes dreams do come true. Meet the vloggers who built multimillion-dollar businesses … from their bedrooms!

Bethany Mota is a hugely successful YouTuber, fashion designer, anti-bullying campaigner, and multimillionaire – and she's still in her twenties. Bethany, an American of Mexican-Portuguese descent, launched her fashion and lifestyle channel, Macbarbie07, at the age of just thirteen. At first, she used her channel as an outlet to overcome the stress of being bullied and to regain her confidence. Only later did she discover the money-making potential of her channel, as fashion companies, realizing she **knew** the younger market **inside out**, started to compete for her collaboration.

Bethany started off specializing in so-called "haul videos," talking about beauty and fashion products she'd just bought. Not until the number of viewers began hitting the thousands, and then the millions, did she realize that such a simple concept would be so successful.

Nobody could call bullying **a blessing in disguise**, but there's no denying that, for Bethany, her experience has led to some incredible opportunities. Never in her wildest dreams did she imagine she'd be interviewing President Obama one day, but that's just one of the many exciting things her fame as a YouTuber has enabled her to do.

In his teens, the Spanish YouTube entrepreneur Samuel de Luque spent a lot of time gaming, which later turned out to be a brilliant career move. Only by playing video games for hours on end could Samuel develop the skills that would enable him to earn a living as a gaming expert.

Unlike Bethany, Samuel did go to college, expecting to have a "practical" career in nursing. However, when he'd finished his training, he started uploading Spanish-language gaming videos to YouTube. At first, this was just for fun, but his videos became wildly successful and attracted millions of followers.

Although, in some ways, his success came **out of the blue**, Samuel undoubtedly has a special talent for what he does. Talking about gaming may sound like **a piece of cake**, but it's his distinctive and exciting narrative style that makes him so popular.

However, it's hard not to be just a little bit envious. Not only does Samuel spend large amounts of time playing games, he also makes money from it. In other words, his hobby has become his career, and that's really what you call having **the best of both worlds**!

B Why do you think Bethany and Samuel were so successful? Do you think you would enjoy their videos?

3 Match the idioms in **bold** in the text with the definitions below.
1 something that is very easy to do   _____
2 something that seems bad at first, but ends up being a benefit   _____
3 the advantages of two different situations   _____
4 completely unexpectedly   _____
5 have very detailed knowledge of something   _____

Go to Vocabulary practice: idioms, page 121

34

adding emphasis (2): inversion and *do/does/did* ▪ idioms   **LANGUAGE**   **4C**

4 **A** Match the two parts of the sentence to make full sentences. Then check your answers in the text.

1 Sometimes dreams do
2 Only later did she
3 Never in her wildest dreams did she
4 Unlike Bethany, Samuel did
5 Only by playing video games for hours on end could Samuel

a discover the money-making potential of her channel.
b imagine she'd be interviewing President Obama.
c go to college.
d come true.
e develop the skills that would enable him to earn a living as a gaming expert.

B Look at the sentences in exercise 4A and answer the questions below. Then read the Grammar box. Which sentences add emphasis by:

1 using the same word order as in questions?   ____ ____ ____
2 adding the auxiliary verb *do/does/did* after the subject ?   ____ ____

📖 **Grammar**   **adding emphasis (2): inversion and *do/does/did***

Inversion after *Never, Not until,* etc.:
Never have I heard *such a story!*
Not until *I became sick **did I realize** how important friends are.*
Only now *that I'm successful **do people take** me seriously!*

do/does/did in affirmative sentences:
Do *take your time reading the instructions*
*Determination **does** count for a lot, after all!*
*He thought the business would fail, but it **did** take off.*

Look! Emphatic *do* is only used in affirmative simple present, simple past, and imperative sentences. In all other forms, the existing auxiliary is stressed for emphasis:
*He **has** been to college. He told me so.*
*Laura **is** in her thirties. I went to her thirtieth birthday celebration.*

Personal Best

Go to **Grammar practice:** adding emphasis (2): inversion and *do/does/did*, page 101

5 **A** ▶ 4.13 **Pronunciation:** sentence stress: emphatic *do/does/did* Listen and pay attention to how emphatic *do/does/did* is stressed.

1 It's true that my sister **does** have a bad temper.
2 Although he denies it, I think he **did** intend to be rude.
3 Ann **did** want to see Jim again. She told me.
4 I'll be amazed if Marco **does** come with us. He never lets his hair down.
5 It's true that these shoes **do** cost a lot, but they're so stylish!
6 I understand, but **do** try to come if you can.

B ▶ 4.13 Listen again and repeat.

6 ▶ 4.14 Listen to Joe and Keira talking about their Internet use. Check (✓) the correct boxes.

Which person says that ...	Joe	Keira	Neither
1 he/she is planning to stop using social media?	☐	☐	☐
2 he/she enjoys reading responses to his/her posts?	☐	☐	☐
3 he/she spends a lot of time answering comments?	☐	☐	☐
4 it's best not to answer negative comments?	☐	☐	☐
5 he/she will post more pictures of his/her cat?	☐	☐	☐
6 people spend too much time on the Internet?	☐	☐	☐
7 he/she uses the Internet to stay in contact with a family member?	☐	☐	☐
8 people often use picture-sharing sites to boast about their lives?	☐	☐	☐

Go to **Communication practice:** Student A page 134, Student B page 145

7 Has the Internet been a help or a hindrance in your life? Do you think it will help you achieve success in the future? In pairs, discuss. Use at least two of the sentence beginnings below.

Rarely ...   Only by ...   Not only ...   No sooner ...   At no time ...   Hardly ... when ...

Only then ...   Never before ...   Not until ...   Under no circumstances ...

Personal Best   Write a paragraph about someone you know who has been successful. Emphasize four pieces of information.

35

4 SKILLS WRITING writing a report ■ formal linkers

4D Progress report

1 Read the definition of "soft skills," and look at the examples below. In pairs, discuss which skills you think you have. Give examples from your studies or professional experience.

soft skills
personal attributes that allow a person to work well with others in a variety of situations

communication skills   leadership   problem solving   critical thinking

team work   flexibility   resilience   negotiation skills   time management

2 Read the progress report below written by Liz, an intern at an architecture company. Which soft skills does she talk about?

Intern Progress Report — Liz Clements

Introduction
The purpose of this report is to evaluate my progress during my first two months at Barker & Jones Architects (BJA), and to suggest areas for further development in order to agree on objectives with my internship manager.

Progress and achievements
During my time at BJA, I feel that I have accomplished a great deal with the help and support of my colleagues. I have fit into the department well, establishing a friendly, yet professional, working relationship with colleagues. Furthermore, I have ensured that my work is well presented and accurate, and I have done my best to meet project targets and deadlines. In addition to this, I feel I have communicated in a clear and professional manner with both colleagues and clients. A notable achievement for me was when my suggested design for an outdoor terrace for the new city library was praised by the client.

Challenges
I have found time management quite challenging. At times I have underestimated how long certain tasks would take, and, consequently, I had insufficient time for subsequent tasks. Nonetheless, I have improved this aspect of my work by setting myself small deadlines for each task. I also found I was spending a large proportion of each day replying to e-mails, which put me behind schedule. I now only reply immediately to important messages, and I set aside half an hour each morning and afternoon to respond to other e-mails. This has been much more time-efficient and has allowed me to be more in control of my time.

Further development
Due to the fact that I will be working more closely on the project schedule, I would welcome the opportunity to learn more about project management. I understand that a training course is offered to staff at BJA, and I would definitely be interested in participating. I look forward to contributing even more effectively to the company by further developing my skills over the forthcoming months.

3 Read Liz's report again and answer the questions.
1. What are the main areas that Liz feels she has progressed in?
2. What has she found difficult?
3. What would she like to develop further?

writing a report ■ formal linkers **WRITING** SKILLS **4D**

Skill | writing a report

The purpose of a report is to inform, instruct, evaluate, and encourage action. A well-written report achieves this purpose by being clear, concise, and appropriate for the reader.
- Divide your report into clear sections. Start with an introduction and finish with suggestions or recommendations for the future.
- Think about who the report is for, and use an appropriate style. A report for a client or person in authority is usually more formal in style than a report for colleagues, which would have a more neutral style.
- Achieve a neutral or formal style by avoiding slang, idioms, exaggeration, and informal expressions. Try to be tactful and polite, and avoid emotional language.

4 Read the Skill box. In pairs, answer the questions below about the report on page 36.
1 Do you think the ideas expressed in the report are clear and concise?
2 What is the purpose of the report?
3 Who was the report written for?
4 Is the style of language used in the report appropriate for the target reader?

5 Read the sentences and underline their more formal equivalents in the report.
1 I'm writing this report to think about how well I've done.
2 I think I've been really successful so far.
3 Everyone here loves me. I get along really well with them all.
4 I was over the moon when the client liked my suggestion!
5 I've had a bit of a tough time organizing my time.
6 Sometimes I thought something would take less time.
7 I didn't have enough time for other things.
8 I'd really love to learn more about …

6 Find two formal-sounding linkers in the second paragraph that mean *also*.

Text builder | formal linkers

In order to connect ideas clearly, we usually use more formal-sounding linkers when writing in a neutral or formal style.

Giving reasons: due/owing to (the fact that), since
Giving results: as a result, therefore, consequently
Talking about purpose: in order to, so as to
Talking about contrast: nevertheless, nonetheless
Giving additional ideas: in addition (to), moreover, furthermore

Due to illness, the office is shut.
I missed the bus. **As a result**, I was late.
We go to sales **so as to** save money.
The exam was hard. **Nonetheless**, I passed it.
It is an effective solution. **Moreover**, it is cheap.

7 Read the Text builder. Replace the words in *italics* in the sentences below with a formal linker.
1 Unfortunately, I made a number of mistakes *because* I was unfamiliar with the procedure.
2 I was unable to attend the first two meetings with the client. *But* I feel I have contributed a great deal to the project.
3 One of my strengths is my resilience. *In addition to this*, I consider myself to be very flexible.
4 I always e-mail my team leader before I leave work *to* update her on my progress.
5 There was a delay with the initial stages of the project, and *so* we found ourselves behind schedule.

8 A PREPARE Think about your job, formal studies, or English course. Make notes about your progress, achievements, challenges, and areas for further development.

B PRACTICE Use the Skill box to write a progress report for your manager, adviser, or teacher. Include appropriate formal language.

C PERSONAL BEST Work in pairs. Exchange your reports. What soft skills has your partner included? Has he/she avoided using informal language?

Personal Best | Imagine you are Liz's manager. Write a paragraph responding to Liz's report on page 36.

3 and 4 REVIEW and PRACTICE

Grammar

1 Complete the sentences with one word.

1. As a child, I _____ spend hours and hours watching cartoons on TV.
2. Rihanna's new music is _____ nearly as good as her previous work.
3. The harder you work, _____ more successful you'll become.
4. Tim puts a lot of effort into his work, but his sister works twice _____ hard.
5. Gas is becoming more _____ more expensive.
6. My cat does nothing _____ sleep all day.
7. It's _____ use talking to Peter. He just won't listen.
8. I regret _____ spent all my money on clothes.
9. _____ only did Carl forget my birthday, he never apologized.
10. No sooner _____ Ann finished one project than she started the next.

2 Use the words in parentheses to complete the sentences so they mean the same as the first sentence.

1. When I was a child, my mother used to tell me to wash my hands.
   When I was a child, my mother _____ to wash my hands. (telling)
2. Your house is much bigger than mine.
   My house _____ as yours. (nowhere)
3. Philadelphia isn't nearly as expensive as New York.
   Philadelphia _____ than New York. (deal)
4. I ran out of time and couldn't finish my homework.
   I didn't _____ my homework. (enough)
5. Trying to convince her is pointless.
   There _____ convince her. (point)
6. I hate it when people tell me what to do.
   I hate _____ to do. (told)
7. I only started to lose weight when I joined a gym.
   Not until _____ to lose weight. (did)
8. This is the most amusing movie I have ever seen.
   Never _____ movie. (such)
9. Would you go on vacation every year as a child?
   _____ every year as a child? (did)
10. The movie started before I got to the theater.
    By the time I _____ started. (already)

3 Choose the correct options to complete the text.

The rise and fall of the moped

In 1974, the United States was in the middle of a serious fuel crisis, and gas was in short supply. In some cities, drivers ¹*would spend / were always spending* hours waiting to fill up their tanks. Most cars were not particularly fuel-efficient back then, so people ²*used to start / had started* looking for a new method of transportation that would enable them ³*to get around / getting around* more efficiently.

The first solution ⁴*to gain / gaining* mainstream acceptance came from Europe, and it was the moped – a hybrid between a bicycle and a motorcycle. Mopeds had very small engines that could not exceed 40 miles an hour, but let owners ⁵*run / to run* more than 200 miles on one tank of gas, which made them ⁶*far / by far* more economical than cars.

Europeans ⁷*were using / had been using* mopeds for decades, but only in the mid 1970s ⁸*they became / did they become* popular in the U.S. In 1977, mopeds took the U.S. market by storm, selling over 250,000 units. Over time, as gas prices eventually dropped, and automobile companies developed more fuel-efficient cars, mopeds fell into oblivion.

Vocabulary

1 Choose the correct options to complete the sentences.

1. CDs *became / went* obsolete years ago.
2. Public speaking doesn't *come / go* easily to most people.
3. The event went according to *plan / planning*.
4. Flared pants went *out of / off* fashion in the 1980s.
5. I *got / took* a wrong turn and got lost.
6. My mother knows me *inside out / upside down*.
7. It's almost 9 p.m. Should we *call / end* it a day?
8. Miranda says she's leaving Michael for *good / always*.

38

REVIEW and PRACTICE 3 and 4

2 Match the two parts of the sentence to make full sentences.

1 I'm sorry I forgot your birthday, but
2 Don't take this the wrong way, but
3 My presentation went over like a lead balloon, which
4 The test was a piece of cake, and
5 It's too soon to make a decision, so
6 I like my career, but

a aren't you too old to be living with your parents?
b family always comes first.
c came as a surprise, since I'd been rehearsing for days.
d I'll make it up to you, I promise.
e let's cross that bridge when we come to it.
f I'm sure I passed with flying colors.

3 Read Jim's journal. Fill in the blanks with a preposition.

The **worst** year ever

JANUARY 2nd: This is going to be the best year ever. I'm going to *fulfill all my goals*, and nothing will [1]hold me _____, especially [2]when it comes _____ my career.

FEBRUARY 8th: I got fired last week. The news came [3]out _____ the blue, and I was shocked. But after a day or two, I realized that losing my job was actually a [4]blessing _____ disguise. I'm sure I'll find something better.

APRIL 4th: I've been out of work for two months. I'm going to have a lot of spare time until I find a job, so I should try to [5]make the best _____ it and work on my French.

MAY 18th: It was getting harder to *make ends meet*, so I asked my sister for a loan. I wasn't sure how she was going to react, but she *took it well*. It [6]goes _____ saying that I intend to pay her back.

JULY 7th: I've had more than ten job interviews, and all I keep hearing is "we'll be in touch soon." Fortunately, I still have some money left [7]_____ the time being.

SEPTEMBER 22nd: I've found a new job! I can work in the office or from home, so it's [8]the best _____ both worlds! And, apparently, they like me, too. My boss told me I'd *exceeded their expectations*.

DECEMBER 12th: The company *went bankrupt* last week. I can't believe it! Instead of making progress, it feels as if I'm [9]going around _____ circles. I've had some pretty bad years [10]_____ my lifetime, but not as bad as this one!

4 Match the expressions in *italics* in exercise 3 with definitions a–e below.

a have enough money to live on
b go out of business; be legally unable to pay
c be better than you thought something would be
d react positively to something
e achieve all my objectives

Personal Best

Lesson 3A — Describe a childhood memory using narrative tenses and the habitual past.

Lesson 3A — Describe a technology that has become obsolete or has evolved, using expressions of time and change.

Lesson 3B — Write two sentences describing something that was going to happen, but has changed.

Lesson 3C — Name six expressions with *come* and *go*.

Lesson 3C — Write four sentences comparing two people you know, using four types of comparatives.

Lesson 3D — Describe an experience from your past using at least two expressions for reminiscing.

Lesson 4A — Write two sentences with infinitives with *to*, two with infinitives without *to*, and two with *-ing* forms.

Lesson 4A — Describe a plan you had that succeeded or one that fell through.

Lesson 4B — Write two conversations using four expressions with *make* and *take*.

Lesson 4C — Give three strong opinions using negative inversion.

Lesson 4C — Write four sentences about a personal experience using different idioms.

Lesson 4D — Write three pairs of sentences. Begin the second one with a formal linker.

UNIT 5

Entertain us!

LANGUAGE ellipsis and substitution ■ tastes and opinions

5A We know what you like

1 **A** Read two comments about entertainment experiences. Complete them with words from the box.

> promising   mediocre   outstanding   appeals   tedious

The comedy night looked ¹_____ as it had a five-star rating from a national newspaper. It went on for three hours, though, so got pretty ²_____ ! Most of the comedians were ³_____ – I hardly laughed at all. Don't waste your money!

☹ 😠   ⧉ Share   👍 Like   💬 Comment

I'd never even heard of *Fargo* before, but Netflix suggested it after I'd watched other black comedy and crime dramas – that kind of TV series really ⁴_____ to me. The acting is ⁵_____ , and the script exceptional. I really recommend it!

❤ 😊   ⧉ Share   👍 Like   💬 Comment

B Have you had any similar experiences? Tell your partner about them.

Go to Vocabulary practice: tastes and opinions, page 122

2 In pairs, tell your partner about:
- an actor you despise or can't face seeing yet again.
- a celebrity who really gets on your nerves.
- a series that sounded promising, but turned out to be average.
- a song you have no desire to listen to.
- a movie with sensational special effects.
- a singer or band you used to be wild about or obsessed with.

3 **A** ▶5.3   Listen to a talk about entertainment recommendations. Are the sentences true (T) or false (F)?

1 The speaker thinks that the amount of choice we have nowadays is overwhelming. _____
2 She thinks that digitally-generated recommendations based on past behavior are always useful. _____
3 The app *Tril* enables friends to recommend entertainment to each other. _____

B In pairs, do you agree with what the speaker says about digitally-generated recommendations? Would you be interested in a peer recommendation app like *Tril*? Why/Why not?

4 **A** Look at the sentences below from the talk. Which words have been omitted (*)? Which words have been substituted by the words in **bold**?

1 Digital algorithms analyze what you buy, * access, and * "like."
2 Computer programs don't really "know" us very well, although they try to *.
3 You once streamed *Beauty and the Beast* for your niece. Do you now have a strong desire to watch every Disney film ever made? Probably **not**.
4 Is there another way to get suggestions? These app developers certainly hope **so**.
5 On *Tril*, you can see which films your friends have watched, but you haven't *.
6 You can choose to view your friends' opinions on *some* forms of entertainment, but not other **ones**.

B In pairs, answer the questions below. Then read the Grammar box.

1 What effect does substituting and omitting words have on the sentences?
2 Can the same words be substituted and omitted in your language?

40

ellipsis and substitution ▪ tastes and opinions | **LANGUAGE** | **5A**

 Grammar ellipsis and substitution

Ellipsis (omitting words)
- after *and*, *but*, *or*, and *then*:
  *I'm really into surfing **and** tennis.*
- after auxiliaries and modals:
  *We haven't finished yet, but Helen **has**.*
- with infinitives:
  *"Should we dance?" "I'd love **to**."*

Substitution
- with *one*(s):
  *The second series was good, but I liked the first **one** best.*
- with *not*:
  *Have you had lunch? If **not**, we can go to a café.*
- with *so*:
  *"Do you think he's back yet?" "I imagine **so**."*

Look! When omitting main verbs, we can change the modal or auxiliary verb, depending on the meaning of the omitted part of the sentence.
*I haven't cleaned up yet, but I really **should** – it's a mess!*
*I haven't cleaned up yet, but I really **can't** – I'm too tired.*

Go to Grammar practice: ellipsis and substitution, page 102

5 A ▶ 5.5 **Pronunciation:** strong and weak forms of *to* Listen and notice the different ways in which the speakers say the word *to*.
1 She asked me if I'd like **to** go skydiving. I said I'd love **to**.
2 He told me **to** read the reviews, but I didn't want **to**.
3 She needs **to** fix her bike, but she doesn't know how **to**.
4 There will be time **to** see the performance, if you'd like **to**.
5 They tried **to** pay for our tickets, but I told them not **to**.
6 I haven't managed **to** see the last season yet, but I hope **to** one day.

B ▶ 5.5 Listen again and repeat.

6 A ▶ 5.6 Listen to Ian and Joanne making recommendations. Are the sentences true (T) or false (F)?
1 Joanne wanted to watch the series *3%* with her boyfriend. ____
2 Ian agrees that the series *3%* can be a little disturbing. ____
3 Ian thinks that Bianca Comparato was good in her last movie. ____
4 Ian wants to go to the hip-hop concert. ____
5 Joanne thinks that Ian would like Sam Smith's music. ____

B ▶ 5.6 Choose the correct options to complete the sentences. Listen and check.
1 My boyfriend suggested watching it together, but I decided *to / not to*.
2 "I've heard it's a little disturbing." "Well, I guess *so / not*."
3 "I loved her in her last movie." "I didn't see that *so / one*."
4 "Do you feel like coming?" "I don't think *to / so*. I'm not a huge fan of hip-hop."
5 I'm working so much right now, so when I'm *to / not*, I need relaxing things in my life!
6 "I've never listened to any of his music, but I'd like *to / so*." "I'm sure you'd love it if you *are / did*."

Go to Communication practice: Student A page 134, Student B page 145

7 Complete the sentences so that they are true for you. In pairs, compare your sentences and respond to what your partner says.

1 When it comes to travel, I have no desire to _____ , but several of my friends do.
2 I'm wild about _____ 's books. You should really read one if you can.
3 The most spectacular show I've ever seen was _____ . Have you seen it or any similar ones?
4 I don't understand why so many people seem to be obsessed with _____ , but apparently they are.
5 The most appalling meal I've had was at _____ . If you were ever thinking of going there, don't!
6 Have you used this fabulous app for _____ ? If not, I'd really recommend it.
7 I've never tried _____ , but I really think I should have – everyone else is obsessed with it.
8 _____ sounded promising, at first. I thought I'd love it, but I don't. The acting is so bad it's tedious!

Personal Best Write a short e-mail to a friend, recommending something you think would appeal to him/her.

41

5 SKILLS READING understanding tone ■ identifying the subject in long sentences

5B Simply a triumph

1 Have you seen any exceptional, average, or disappointing movies lately? In pairs, discuss.

2 Read the three movie reviews on page 43. Is each review generally positive or negative?

> **Skill understanding tone**
>
> **Evaluating tone helps us understand the writer's attitude toward the subject.**
> - Tone can be admiring, critical, disappointed, informative, objective, persuasive, sarcastic, serious, etc.
> - Tone can change within the text.
> - To identify tone, look for clues in the writer's choice of language. An admiring tone can be conveyed by words such as *stunning, amazing, breath-taking*. A disappointed tone can be conveyed by words and phrases such as *lacking, doesn't live up to, fails to*.

3 Read the Skill box. Find phrases and sentences in the reviews that mean the following:

1 isn't as good as it sounded.
2 the acting is good, but there's no suspense or surprises.
3 in the future, people will think it's one of the best movies of its type.
4 the acting makes this movie particularly good.
5 it begins well, but quickly deteriorates.
6 almost everything else in the movie is poor.

4 Choose two adjectives that describe the tone of each review.

1 *The Circle*: disappointed   humorous   critical
2 *Blade Runner 2049*: admiring   persuasive   unconvinced
3 *If You Saw His Heart*: serious   sarcastic   unimpressed

5 Read the reviews again. Match the sentences with the movies. Sometimes there are two answers.

1 The reviewer thought the story was inadequate.
2 The reviewer liked the background music in this movie.
3 This movie features a character that viewers may already be familiar with.
4 This movie explores current themes from real life.
5 Parts of this movie are set in a time before the main story begins.
6 The reviewer praises the production quality of this movie.

> **Text builder identifying the subject in long sentences**
>
> **To identify the subject, look for the verb in the main clause. The subject will be before this. Be careful, there may be information between the subject and the verb, and the subject may be one word, a pronoun, or a noun phrase.**
> *Set in Los Angeles, <u>the movie</u>, which takes place 30 years after the original Blade Runner, <u>features</u> Ryan Gosling as LAPD officer K, a limited-lifespan replicant (android) tasked with tracking down and destroying the original replicants.*

6 A Read the Text builder. Then identify the subject in the first sentence of each review.

B <u>Underline</u> the subject of the sentences below.

1 After suffering years of mistreatment at the hands of her stepmother, eleven-year-old Jennie, in a wonderful performance by newcomer Evie O'Neill, runs away in search of happiness.
2 Keeping viewers not just entertained, but captivated for over three hours is a remarkable achievement by Colombian director Alonso Ramírez.
3 Despite a huge budget and a cast featuring various Oscar nominees, the movie, which felt dull and unoriginal, was one of the year's biggest disappointments.

7 Discuss the movies with a partner. If you have seen them, do you agree with the reviews? If not, do the reviews make you want to see them or do they put you off?

understanding tone ■ identifying the subject in long sentences   READING   SKILLS   5B

The Circle ★★★☆☆

Set in today's social media-dominated age, with people growing more and more concerned about their digital footprints, the premise of *The Circle* feels perfectly relevant. Starring Emma Watson, following on from the phenomenal success of *Beauty and the Beast*, and John Boyega, in his first role since *Star Wars: The Force Awakens*, the movie sounds extremely promising. Unfortunately, *The Circle* fails to live up to its promise.

Watson stars as Mae, a twenty-something stuck in an uninspiring job until her life is transformed when she starts working for the powerful Internet company The Circle, whose technological innovations champion transparency at the expense of privacy. Co-founder Eamon (Tom Hanks) takes a strong interest in Mae. Yet she soon realizes that all is not as it seems after encountering a mysterious colleague (Boyega).

The movie successfully captures the feeling of the modern digital era, dealing with extreme uses of technology, and forcing us to consider uncomfortable questions about privacy and surveillance. Despite this, the story feels underdeveloped, and the relationships between characters are shallow, with no satisfying outcome. While the performances are solid, the movie fails to build up intrigue, and the action feels very predictable. Ultimately, *The Circle* leaves the viewer with the feeling that it could have been considerably better.

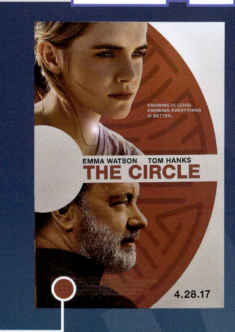

Blade Runner 2049 ★★★★★

Creating a successful sequel to the original and phenomenally successful *Blade Runner* movie, directed by Ridley Scott and starring Harrison Ford, was always going to be a mammoth test. But *Blade Runner 2049* passes with flying colors. It is, quite simply, a triumph, and will surely be considered a classic of the genre for many years to come.

Set in Los Angeles, the movie, which takes place 30 years after the original *Blade Runner*, features Ryan Gosling as LAPD officer K, a limited-lifespan replicant (android) tasked with tracking down and destroying the original replicants. K goes on a dangerous mission, leading him to meet officer Rick Deckard, a role played by Harrison Ford.

The production and cinematography are awe-inspiring, as is the score. Stunning computer-generated imagery makes the movie utterly compelling, and sensational to watch on the big screen. But it is the acting which really takes this movie to a whole other level, with wonderful performances from all the leads, plus virtual Hollywood-newcomer Ana de Armas is delightful as K's love interest, Joi. All in all, *Blade Runner 2049* is an exceptional spectacle that manages to be simultaneously satirical, tragic, and romantic. Not to be missed.

If You Saw His Heart (Si Tu Voyais Son Coeur) ★★☆☆☆

With its two lead characters played by Marine Vacth and Gael García Bernal, and a brilliantly shot opening scene at a raucous wedding, *If You Saw His Heart* starts off impressively. However, things go swiftly downhill. The plot reveals itself to be paper thin, and many of the supporting characters have about as much point as a blunt pencil. While pretty to look at, it's definitely a case of style over substance.

García Bernal plays Daniel, a petty thief hiding out in a rundown hotel, on the run from his best friend's psychotic older brother. The movie features frequent flashbacks to traumatic events in his past. (Daniel feels guilty for turning his friend into a criminal, which led to his accidental death.) When the captivating Francine (Vacth) checks into the hotel, she predictably becomes García Bernal's romantic interest. Yet by this time, the audience couldn't really care less.

The cinematography is good, and it does well in creating an atmosphere, but the movie is sadly lacking in almost every other respect. The romance between the two leads is about as interesting as watching paint dry. *If You Saw His Heart* could be an intriguing movie, but, to be brutally honest, it lacks a heart, and I will have forgotten about it by the time I finish writing this sentence.

Personal Best Write a paragraph reviewing a movie you have seen.

5 LANGUAGE — noun phrases ■ verb suffixes

5C Standing out

1 What kind of appearance, personality, and behavior do you associate with conventional people? What about eccentric people? In pairs, discuss.

2 A Look at the photos in the article below. Who are these people? What do you think makes them eccentric? Read the article quickly and check.

B Read the article again and choose the best summary.

1 Eccentric people often work in the entertainment industry. We are all eccentric in our own way, so we like entertainers who are eccentric, too.
2 Celebrities are often more popular if they are eccentric, even if they do something unpleasant. However, this is only true when the public believes their eccentricity is genuine.

The weirdness effect

Want to make a name for yourself in the creative and entertainment industries? Talent and hard work are essential, as is a generous dose of luck. But, according to experts, it also helps to be a little unusual!

Studies by Dr. Eric Igou and Dr. Wijnand van Tilburg suggest that we're often more attracted to artists and performers who behave eccentrically, maybe because we associate unusual behavior with creativity. They found that people preferred Lady Gaga's music after they'd seen the singer in a masked outfit, as opposed to more conventional clothing. This "weirdness effect" was even apparent for fictional artists. A group shown a photo of an unshaven man with long hair thought "his work" was better than the group shown a neatly-dressed man.

Strangely – and maybe worryingly – this response extended not only to external features such as clothing or style, but even to evidence of seriously disturbed behavior. Apparently, viewers of Van Gogh's still-life *Sunflowers* rated it more highly if they'd been told that the artist had cut off his own ear!

Of course, each of us is eccentric in our own way. There's no such thing as a completely average person, and research suggests that trying to minimize our own differences may even be bad for us. It seems that people who aren't afraid of standing out from the crowd are often more creative, optimistic, and even healthier than those who prefer to blend in.

However, this certainly doesn't justify growing a Salvador Dalí mustache, changing your name to an unpronounceable symbol like Prince, or wearing weird and wonderful outfits like Björk – unless you really want to! Igou and van Tilburg's studies also showed that when people exaggerate their "weirdness" for attention, their appeal is weakened. The moral of the story seems to be: dare to be different, but always be yourself.

3 In pairs, answer the questions.
1 To what extent do you agree (or disagree) with the writer?
2 Which other celebrities do you consider eccentric? Does their eccentricity add to their appeal?

4 Look at the last two paragraphs of the article. Find four verbs with the following infinitive endings:
1 -ate _____   2 -en _____   3 -ify _____   4 -ize _____

Go to Vocabulary practice: verb suffixes, page 122

5 A Complete the noun phrases from the article with the main noun of each phrase.
1 a generous _____ of luck
2 Lady Gaga's _____
3 a completely average _____
4 _____ who aren't afraid of standing out from the crowd
5 the _____ of the story

noun phrases ■ verb suffixes   **LANGUAGE** **5C**

B Match the noun phrases in exercise 5A with forms a–e below. Then read the Grammar box.

Which main noun comes:
a after a noun with a possessive *'s*?   _____
b after an adjective and before a prepositional phrase?   _____
c after an adverb and an adjective?   _____
d before a possessive *of*?   _____
e before a clause?   _____

📖 Grammar   noun phrases

Information after the noun
Phrases with prepositions, *-ing* forms,
infinitives, and clauses:
*We drank <u>water</u> **from the river**.*
*I saw <u>Jan</u> **waving**.*
*I have <u>plans</u> **to make money**.*
*There are <u>rumors</u> **that he's in jail**.*

Information before the noun
Determiners, adverbs, and adjectives:
*It was **an amazingly beautiful** <u>sunset</u>.*

Information before and after the noun:
*I need **some** <u>advice</u> **on fashion**.*
*Who's **that** <u>man</u> **playing the electric guitar**?*

With possessive *'s* or *of*:
*Jon's **first** <u>reaction</u> was to scream.*
*It's **the** <u>title</u> **of his autobiography**.*

Noun + noun compounds:
*She lost her **glasses** <u>case</u>.*
*I have a reusable **coffee** <u>cup</u>.*

Look! Using noun phrases helps us combine information in a more fluent and concise way.
*He's **the highly talented** <u>director</u> **of that hilarious romantic comedy I told you about**.*

Personal Best

Go to Grammar practice: noun phrases, page 103

6 ▶5.9 **Pronunciation:** word stress in compound nouns <u>Underline</u> the stressed syllable in the compound nouns in **bold**. Then listen and repeat.

1 I need a socket to plug in my **phone charger**.
2 We bought some plants at the **garden center**.
3 I can't find the **can opener** anywhere.
4 We watched a **comedy show** on TV last night.
5 Put on your **seat belt**. It's compulsory to wear one.
6 The police found her fingerprints all over the **crime scene**.

7 A ▶5.10 Listen to three people talking about eccentric people they know. What eccentric things do they do?

B ▶5.10 Listen again and complete the noun phrases with one or two words.

1 The most eccentric person I know is a guy _____ in the same _____ as me.
2 He loves going barefoot so he can feel the _____ textures of _____ he walks on.
3 My _____ Eddie's _____ Marisa is pretty quirky.
4 We're tricked into wanting them by the _____ campaigns _____ that just want our money.
5 She dyes her hair a _____ shade of bright _____ green.
6 She even has a huge piece of _____ plastic _____ the window of her bedroom.

Go to Communication practice: Student A page 135, Student B page 145

8 In pairs, take the quiz below.

When was the last time you:

- watched the sun setting over a beautiful landscape?
- prepared a delicious homemade meal for someone?
- heard waves crashing against the seashore?
- saw someone doing something that made you laugh?

- got together with an old friend you hadn't seen for ages?
- were impressed by the courage of someone you know?
- spoke to a person who brightened up your day?

Personal Best Write a short description of a place you love. Use at least four noun phrases of three words or more.

45

5 SKILLS SPEAKING speculating ■ using repetition

5D Everything changes

1 Answer the questions below about the following places in your local area.

independent stores

(movie) theaters and music venues

cafés and restaurants

1 How many of these places are there? Which is your favorite of each? Why?
2 How long have they been there? Have any opened or closed down recently?

2 5.11 Watch or listen to the first part of *Talking Zone* and answer the questions.

1 What is closing down in Ben and Abigail's local area?
2 Why is it closing down, according to Ben and Abigail?

3 5.11 Complete the conversations with the words in the box. Watch or listen again and check.

> unlikely doubt reckon probability guess slim

Abigail My ¹_____ is that it's struggling to make money since all those huge new Megaplexes opened.
Ben I ²_____ you're right. I'm really not a fan of those places.
***
Abigail I wonder whether it might reopen?
Ben I'd say that's ³_____ . I guess there's a ⁴_____ chance they'll keep the building, but I ⁵_____ they'll reopen it as a cinema.
***
Abigail What's left? The Screen on Green Street?
Ben Yeah, although, in all ⁶_____ , that will end up closing soon, too.

Conversation builder | speculating

Expressions to use when we're not 100% sure about something
*I suppose …   I wonder whether …   I guess … / My guess is …   I bet … / You can bet that …
I doubt …   Presumably …   There's no / a slim chance that …   Chances are that …
I imagine …   In all probability …   I wouldn't be surprised if …   I'd say …*

Modals and modal-like verbs used for speculating
*It might …   They could have …   She can't have …   He must …   It's likely …
It's unlikely …   I assume …*

4 A Read the Conversation builder. Complete the chart with expressions from the builder box.

Impossible or improbable	Possible or probable
I doubt …	Chances are that …

B How likely do you think these things are? Discuss in pairs. Use expressions from exercise 4A.

1 Humans will live on the Moon in the near future.
2 My country will win the next soccer World Cup.
3 You got up early this morning.
4 Everyone in this class has a smartphone.

speculating ■ using repetition **SPEAKING**   SKILLS **5D**

5 A ▶ 5.12 Watch or listen to the second part of the show. Answer the questions.
1 What other changes in the city do Ben and Abigail talk about?
2 What do they disagree about?

B ▶ 5.12 Complete each of the second sentences with one word. Watch or listen again and check.

1	**Ben**	That new film *Eva* came out today.
	Abigail	Really? *Eva* came out _____ ?
2	**Abigail**	Do you want to see that one instead?
	Ben	_____ of the Coen Brothers film?
3	**Ben**	Past the theater and down by Wiltons.
	Abigail	_____ ? The old music store?
4	**Abigail**	It closed down, too.
	Ben	It _____ down? Are you serious?
5	**Abigail**	What I'm trying to say is ... what I'm _____ to say is that just because something is new, doesn't make it bad.

Skill using repetition

When speaking, we use repetition for various purposes:

- to clarify
  - **A** Which do you prefer: New York or Los Angeles?
  - **B** Which do I prefer as a place to live? Or to go on vacation?

- to correct
  - **A** We still have half an hour 'til the train comes, don't we?
  - **B** Half an hour? No, we've got less than ten minutes!

- to show interest
  - **A** My sister has a new job working for the local government.
  - **B** Working for the local government? Is she enjoying it?

- to show surprise
  - **A** I was so angry with Gillian I just hung up on her.
  - **B** You hung up on her? That's not like you to be so rude!

- to give yourself time to think
  - **A** Could you tell us about a challenge you've overcome?
  - **B** A challenge I've overcome ... oh yes, I know. Last week ...

6 Read the Skill box. Identify the reason for repetition for each example in exercise 5B.

7 A ▶ 5.13 Complete the responses with the number of words in parentheses. Listen and check.

1 **A** What's your favorite time of day?
  B (five words)? Hmm ... probably late morning.
2 **A** Well, that was a really interesting film.
  B (one word)? I fell asleep it was so boring!
3 **A** I expected a refund, but I got nothing.
  B (one word)? Like, zero? That's ridiculous!
4 **A** Loris is the best student in my class.
  B (two words)? As in the most hard-working?
5 **A** I have to write an essay on marketing this week.
  B (four words)? What's the essay title?

B Why do the speakers in 7A use repetition? Practice the conversations with a partner.

Go to Communication Practice: Student A page 135, Student B page 146

8 A **PREPARE** Make notes on how you would answer the questions.
1 How do you think your city will change in your lifetime? Which places will close down?
2 Which buildings will still exist? What new facilities will there be?

B **PRACTICE** Discuss the questions in pairs. Speculate and use repetition to clarify, show interest, etc.

C **PERSONAL BEST** Think about how well you answered the questions. Did you speculate about things you thought would and wouldn't happen? Did you use repetition appropriately? Find a new partner and ask and answer the questions again.

Personal Best Write a paragraph that speculates about you and your friends in ten years.

GRAMMAR PRACTICE

1A The present: simple, continuous, and perfect aspects

 1.5

Good weather **cheers** us up.
I**'m** just **walking** out the door now.
I still **haven't received** my exam results.
She**'s been studying**, so she turned off her phone.

Aspect adds meaning to the verb form. The **continuous aspect** can add meaning about the duration of an action. The action is viewed at some point between its start and end, and can mean that it is in progress and temporary. The **perfect aspect** can mean the action is completed, or has an effect on a later situation. The **simple aspect** doesn't usually add meaning, but can express facts.

Simple present
We use the simple present to talk about routines and facts. We often use the simple present with frequency adverbs and expressions.

It snows frequently in the winter here.
My younger brother annoys me most of the time.

Present continuous
We use the present continuous to talk about actions that are in progress or temporary at the moment. We can use *just* to emphasize "now."

He's living with his parents, but he'll get his own place soon.
I'm just putting dinner in the oven.

We can also use the present continuous with *always* to talk about things that happen frequently, especially things that are annoying.

You're always leaving the top off the toothpaste tube!

Some verbs, such as *think*, *have*, and *feel*, can be both action and state verbs, with different meanings. When they are action verbs, we can use the present continuous, but when they are state verbs, we can only use the simple present.

I'm having some doubts about my new boyfriend. (the action of having)
I have three really great teachers this semester. (the state of having)

Present perfect
We use the present perfect to talk about past experiences or actions without specifying when they happened. The actions are usually complete.

We've won the championship many times.
I've read that novel.

We also use the present perfect to talk about actions or states that start in the past and continue in the present, or past actions that have an effect on the present.

How long have you belonged to this club? I've been a member for 15 years.
She's moved away. She's now living in San Francisco.

Present perfect continuous
We use the present perfect continuous to talk about longer, repeated actions that are still taking place, or have recently finished. It can also show that the action has an effect on the present.

I've been painting all morning. (I'm still painting, or I've recently completed it.)
I'm covered in paint because I've been painting. (effect of action: I'm covered in paint.)

1 Choose the correct options to complete the sentences.
   1 They *are living / live* at Anna's house for a few weeks.
   2 Jake*'s having / has* lunch in the cafeteria every other Wednesday.
   3 Our boss *is always talking / always talks* about our sales figures. It's so annoying!
   4 The number of people in their sixties *has been increasing / has increased* by five percent since last year.
   5 She *just sends / is just sending* me the information, so we'll have it soon.
   6 I *'ve been saving / 've saved* money for a vacation, but so far I've *saved / been saving* only $200.
   7 Where *are you calling / do you call* from? It's hard to hear you.
   8 Laura is still studying for her exam. In fact, she *'s been studying / 's studied* all night.

2 Check (✓) the sentences if they are correct, or correct any mistakes.
   1 He's working in a bank for the last ten years.
   2 Have you finished your assignment for tomorrow?
   3 I watch a series called *Run!* right now.
   4 We've been painting the bedroom all morning.
   5 They live in Madrid since last month.
   6 You're always following celebrities on Instagram.
   7 I wait ages to hear from you.
   8 Evidence shows that the Earth's climate changes in recent years.

3 Complete the text with the correct form of the verbs in parentheses. There may be more than one answer.

   Languages [1]_____ (always, change) and evolving to adapt to speakers' needs. Some [2]_____ (evolve) more quickly than others. In the case of English, older generations often complain about the poor standard of young people's English, that we [3]_____ (always, use) text-speak and incorrect grammar. Anyway, while any change is barely noticeable from year to year, it [4]_____ (become) more apparent in texts from decades or centuries ago. I [5]_____ (read) some of Shakespeare's most famous works over the past few weeks, and I [6]_____ (find) the English incomprehensible on many occasions! Also, my family and I [7]_____ (discover) my grandmother's journals. It's interesting to see old-fashioned words, like "settee" instead of "sofa" (By the way, my mom [8]_____ (call) it a "couch"!).

◀ Go back to page 5

94

1C Adding emphasis (1): cleft sentences

 1.8

It was my grandmother who was the most important influence in my life.
It's my biology teacher I really respect.
What you need is a good vacation.
What shocked him were the text messages he received.
The person I really want to see is my old professor.

Adding emphasis with *It*

We use cleft sentences to emphasize part of a sentence. We form a cleft sentence with *It* + a past or present form of *be* + the focus word + a *who/that* clause.

It was my father who/that inspired me to be a doctor. (*My father* is the subject of the sentence.)

In a cleft sentence where we emphasize the subject, the relative pronoun *who* or *that* cannot be omitted.

It's my sister who taught me how to think for myself. NOT *It's my sister taught me how to think for myself.*

We can also emphasize the object of the sentence. The relative pronoun is optional. The object may also be the object of a preposition.

It's my history professor (who/that) I admire the most. (*My history professor* is the object of the sentence.)
It was my older brother (who/that) I always did things with. (*My older brother* is the object of the preposition *with*.)

Sometimes we use cleft sentences to correct information.

It wasn't my father who gave me the money. It was my brother who lent it to me.

Look! Even if the subject of the sentence is plural, we use *It's* or *It was*.
It was our grandparents who raised us.

Adding emphasis with *What*

We can also add emphasis by beginning a sentence with *What*. We can emphasize a noun, or we can emphasize a clause.

What interests me the most is art. = Art interests me the most.
What I really want is to run the marathon. = I really want to run the marathon.

We can use *The (main) thing that* instead of *What*.

What/The (main) thing that annoys me is the amount of traffic.
What/The (main) thing (that) I worry about is the increase in prices.

When the noun is plural, we use a plural form of *be*.

What I really like are the chocolate chips in the middle.

Adding emphasis with *The person who*, etc.

We can add emphasis by beginning a sentence with phrases such as *The person who/that*, *The thing that*, *The reason why*, and *The place that*.

The person who helped me most was my sister.
The place (that) you really should visit is Vietnam.
The reason (why) I called her was to say good-bye.

We can also add emphasis with the phrases *All (that)* and *The only thing (that)*.

All (that)/The only thing (that) I want is to speak freely.
All we need is love.

GRAMMAR PRACTICE

1 Match the two parts of the sentences.
   1 What I wanted to say
   2 The main thing
   3 It was my best friend
   4 The person I really want to thank
   5 What concerns me most
   6 The reason I'm here
   7 It was the final part of the story
   8 What you need

   a that I didn't really understand.
   b is some medicine and an early night.
   c is that everyone tries to cooperate.
   d is that I am very grateful for everyone's support.
   e is to explain the new sales strategy.
   f is the lack of safety equipment.
   g is my old math teacher.
   h who helped me find a new apartment.

2 Complete the second sentences so they have the same meaning as the first sentences.
   1 I just need a few minutes to think about it.
     All I _____ .
   2 I wanted to speak to my brother and nobody else.
     The only _____ .
   3 The number of homeless children worries us.
     What _____ .
   4 The IT specialist told me about the hacker stealing my personal details.
     It _____ the IT specialist _____ .
   5 I really want to visit Venice next year.
     The place _____ .
   6 Lynn forgot to buy the tickets.
     It _____ Lynn _____ .
   7 You have to start reviewing now before it's too late.
     The main _____ you _____ .
   8 How dirty our streets are bothers me.
     What _____ .
   9 I got tired of the third season of that series.
     It _____ .

◀ Go back to page 9

GRAMMAR PRACTICE

2A Modal verbs (1) and modal-like forms

 2.4

You **ought to** ask Sophie what she thinks.
He **managed to** complete the race despite his injury.
You **should** be back at work within a week or so.
You're **not supposed to** eat just before bedtime.
You **need to** return this form before the end of the month.

Advice and recommendation: *had better, have to, ought to*

We use *had better* (*not*) to express strong advice that can warn against a negative result.

You'd better go or you'll be late.
He'd better not forget my birthday this year!

We use *have to* (affirmative) and *can't* (negative) to give strong advice about something urgent. We use *ought to* to give advice or make a recommendation.

Tell James he can't forget to bring his identity card.
We really ought to leave now.

We also use *have to* to recommend something very strongly to someone because we are certain he/she will like it.

Millie, you have to go to Café Espresso – you'll absolutely love it!

Ability and willingness: *manage to, be prepared/willing to*

We use *manage to* to say that we succeed in doing something difficult.

We actually manage to eat pretty well on thirty dollars a week.
I didn't manage to persuade Dan to pay for the trip.

We can use *be prepared to* to say we are willing to do something challenging or requiring effort.

I'm (even) prepared to move if that's what it takes to get a job.

We generally use *not willing to* for things that we find unacceptable.

I'm not willing to wait six months for an appointment. It's just ridiculous.

Possibility and speculation: *be likely to, should, may*

We use *be likely to* to say that something will probably happen.

He's likely to be away for at least a week.

We use *should* to say that we think that something is true, or we expect that something will happen.

Emily should be there by now.
His health should improve if he maintains the diet.

We use *may* or *might* to speculate about what is possible.

She may have an allergy that we don't know about.
William might be perfectly happy to stay at home.

Obligation and necessity: *need to, be supposed to*

We use *need to* to talk about something that is necessary.

She needs to work a little harder.

We use *be supposed to* to talk about expected obligation. We can also use it to talk about something that rules or instructions tell us we should do.

You're supposed to rest. You're not supposed to exercise after eating.

---

1 Choose the correct options to complete the sentences.

1 We have to be there for the start of the ceremony, so you really *ought to / can't* be late.
2 You *had better / have to* see them in concert, Sam – they're absolutely fantastic.
3 I don't know why Sara's not here today. She *may / should* be sick, I suppose.
4 My grandfather *is / isn't* supposed to drink coffee, but he does anyway.
5 I'm not willing *working / to work* twelve hours a day. It's too much.
6 If you'd like to contribute some money for Jack's gift you can, but you *must not / don't need to*.
7 I don't know how we did it, but somehow we managed *fitting / to fit* everything in the back of the car.
8 If you miss the seven o'clock train, the next train will be too late, so you really *can't / don't need to* miss it.
9 I don't know what's causing the problem. It *should / might* be that a pipe is blocked.
10 People who exercise regularly *are less likely / ought not* to suffer from so many common colds.

2 Complete the second sentences so they have the same meaning as the first sentences, using the correct form of the modals in the box.

| be allowed to   be prepared to   manage to |
| had better   have to   not need to   supposed to |

1 Luckily, I succeeded in getting to the store just before it closed.
   Luckily, I _____.
2 This software is expensive, but I'm willing to try it out.
   This software is expensive, but I _____.
3 This milk doesn't smell right. We should throw it away.
   This milk doesn't smell right. We _____.
4 You can rent ski equipment at the resort, so taking it with you isn't necessary.
   You can rent ski equipment at the resort, so you _____.
5 Can we take photographs inside the building?
   Are we _____?
6 I really think you should try my gym, Adam – it's so good.
   You _____.
7 You should be studying, not chatting online!
   You're _____.

◀ Go back to page 13

96

2C Modal verbs (2): advanced forms

 2.12

Mira **should be spending** time with people her own age.
Tom **might** not even **be going** to the party.
They **might have refused** to lend Laura money. They didn't say.
I **needn't have worried** about Alex because he wasn't upset.
Sophie **can't have been** more than three in that photo.
Jack **may have been trying** to make me feel better! He said he liked my talk.
I **should have been studying** at home, but I went to Isabel's party.

Continuous

We use modal verbs in the continuous form (modal + *be* + *-ing* form of the main verb) to talk about what is happening now.

You shouldn't be spending all your money on going out.
Surely she can't be studying at four o'clock in the morning!

Sometimes we can say the same sentence with a more general meaning using the simple form of the modal verb (modal + base form of the main verb).

You shouldn't spend all your money on going out. (= in general)
Surely she can't study at four o'clock in the morning! (= in general)

Perfect

We use modal verbs in the perfect form (modal + *have* + past participle form of the main verb) to talk about the past.

We had tons of food. I needn't have worried that we wouldn't have enough.
Jamie didn't come to work yesterday. He must have been sick.

We also use modal verbs in the perfect form to talk about things that didn't happen.

The portions were so small. I could have eaten twice that amount (but I didn't).
I didn't tell Zoe. She would have been really angry if she'd known (but she didn't).

> **Look!** We use *needn't have* or *didn't need to* when we want to talk about things that weren't necessary. We often use *actually* or *really* before *didn't need to* when we realize this after we've already done something. *Needn't have* is more formal than *didn't need to*.
> *My train was late. I needn't have rushed to get to the station./My train was late. I actually didn't need to rush to get to the station.*

Perfect continuous

We use modal verbs in the perfect continuous form (modal + *have been* + *-ing* form of the main verb) to talk about things that were happening or true at a point in time in the past.

I don't know what she was doing in Lima. She may have been visiting a friend.
You should have been listening to your teacher instead of talking!
When she mentioned Mr. Taylor, she can't have been referring to her son, could she?

The perfect continuous sometimes emphasizes the continuous nature of the action, and it can also emphasize the meaning "at that point in time."

You should have been listening to your teacher (during the whole class).
She can't have been referring to her son (at that point in time).

In the perfect and perfect continuous forms, we do not change *have* or *have been* to *has* or *has been* in the third person singular. It is always in the infinitive form.

He really shouldn't have been driving if he was so tired. NOT *He really shouldn't has been driving if he was so tired.*

GRAMMAR PRACTICE

1 Correct any mistakes in the form of the modal verbs in *italics*.

1. She certainly said she had the right qualifications for the job, although I suppose she *may have been lying*.
2. We *could have invited* George and Alfie to the party, but we were trying to keep the numbers down.
3. Nicola only changed jobs last year. She *can't to be looking* for another job already!
4. Noah's bike is still here. He *must be walking* to the station.
5. Oh no – there's no cheese left. Laura *must have been eating* it all.
6. You *shouldn't be reviewing* for a test right now. You're exhausted.
7. In the end, Julia got a ride to the airport with Ethan, so she *can't have taken* the bus.
8. I wish I'd spoken to James. I *should have been calling* him last night and explained the problem.

2 Complete the sentences with the correct form of the word in parentheses.

1. They're certainly not here now. They must _____ already. (leave)
2. I wonder why Luke didn't hear the burglars enter his apartment. I guess he could _____ at the time. (sleep)
3. I'm not surprised you were angry with William. If I were you, I would _____ furious. (be)
4. I wonder where Olivia was going when we saw her. She can't _____ home as she was headed east, but lives on the other side of town. (go)
5. Sarah and John are packing the car. They must _____ ready to go on vacation. (get)
6. I didn't tell Ryan it was my birthday. He would _____ me a present, and I know he can't afford it. (buy)
7. I don't know if Sophie will want any food this evening. She might _____ already. (eat)
8. You're sick! Get inside where it's warm! You shouldn't _____ in the cold and the rain! (walk)

"You needn't have done the dishes. We have a new dishwasher!"

◀ Go back to page 17

GRAMMAR PRACTICE

3A Past time

 3.4

I **was jogging** along Green Lane when I **saw** her.
Jess and Mark **had** already **left** by the time we **arrived**.
Strangely enough, I**'d been thinking** about Lily when she **called**.
My parents **used to throw** really big parties once or twice a year.
She **didn't use to** wear her hair so short when she **was** younger.
We **would** often see her on our way to school.
I **was always begging** my mother for a pet.

Past narration

In a narrative, we often use a variety of tenses. We use the past continuous to describe background events, and to describe an action that was already in progress when another action happened.

It was freezing cold and snowing, so we decided to stay in.
I was just having coffee when I got a call from Oscar.

We often use *when*, *while*, and *before* to connect events.

When I got on the train, I saw my old boyfriend out of the corner of my eye.
While I was waiting for Thomas to arrive, I e-mailed my mom.

We use the past perfect to describe an action that happened before another action in the past. We often connect past events with *before* or *by the time*.

We offered to help, but the problem had already been fixed.
By the time I got there, Dylan had already left.

We use the past perfect continuous to set the scene or to describe an action in progress in the past before another action occurred.

I'd been thinking of changing jobs when I got this offer.
It had been snowing most of the day, and there was a foot of snow on the ground.

Habitual past

Past habitual forms often have similar meanings, and we vary them to avoid repetition. We use *used to*, *would*, and the simple past to talk about states or habits in the past.

I used to hate broccoli when I was a child, and I would hide it under the table and pretend I'd eaten it! It always drove my mom crazy!

When *used to* is in the negative or question form, we use *use to* without a *d*, like other simple past verbs.

She didn't use to talk very much in class. NOT *She didn't used to talk very much in class.*
Did Mom use to look like me when she was my age? NOT *Did Mom used to look like me when she was my age?*

We can't use *would* to describe states. Instead, we use *used to* or the simple past.

I used to be/was in a lot better shape when I was younger. NOT *I would be in a lot better shape when I was younger.*

We can also use the past continuous with *always* for describing things that happened repeatedly, especially when they were annoying.

Tom was never happy – he was always complaining about something.
I never really liked Beth. She was always bossing us around.

---

1 Choose the correct options to complete the sentences. Where both options are possible, (circle) both.

1 The first thing I noticed when I stepped off the plane was how green everywhere was. You could see it *rained / had been raining* for weeks.
2 The only thing I can remember about Zoe is that she *was / would be* crazy about horses.
3 By the time I met James, he was pretty lonely because both of his sons *had gone / went* to live in Australia.
4 Did you *used to / use to* see much of your grandparents when you were little?
5 It was funny that Jacob mentioned working vacations. I *had been reading / read* an article on the subject that day.
6 I *drew / used to draw* a lot when I was a child.
7 My sister and I *used to / would* read to each other at bedtime.
8 I saw a woman chasing a man down the street, yelling "Thief!" I assumed that he *stole / had stolen* her bag.
9 People *didn't use to / used to* travel as much in those days.
10 Every morning, before class started, we *would / used to* get coffee together.

2 Correct the five mistakes in the text. Sometimes two answers are possible.

> My favorite childhood memories are of vacations spent with my grandparents. My brother and I loved staying with our grandparents in their old cottage. Winter vacations were especially magical because they would live in a part of the country where it snowed a lot. It was cold, because my grandparents didn't used to put the central heating on, but my grandma would light a fire in the living room so that we could gather around it and get warm. I remember one morning very vividly. We got up to find that it was snowing all night. My grandpa couldn't even open the back door because the wind blew the snow against it, and it formed a thick, white wall. My brother and I were so excited, imagining that we were trapped!

98 ◀ Go back to page 23

3C Comparison

 3.9

The new treatment will be **considerably more expensive than** existing treatments.
His new novel is**n't nearly as complex as** his previous one.
The more I see him, **the less** I like him, to be honest.
Her health's just getting **worse and worse**.

Modifying comparisons

We use *far*, (*very*) *much*, *somewhat*, and *a good/great deal* before comparative adjectives or adverbs to express a moderate to big difference.

This hotel is far more expensive than the last one we stayed in.
He runs a good deal faster than I do.

Some modifiers, such as *way* and *a lot*, are informal. We avoid them in formal speech or writing, and use *considerably* or *a great deal*, instead.

She's way smarter! She's a great deal more intelligent.
Dan looks a lot older. Dan looks considerably older.

We use *slightly* and *a little* before comparative adjectives or adverbs to express a small difference. We can also use the more informal expression *a bit*.

Her hair is slightly darker than yours.
Thankfully, my computer is running a bit more quickly this morning.

When we make comparisons with nouns, we can express a big difference by adding *much*, *far*, or *a lot* for uncountable nouns and *many*, *far*, or *a lot* for countable nouns.

I used to eat much more chocolate when I was younger. (= uncountable)
I get a lot more colds these days. (= countable)

We can express a small difference by using *a little* or *a bit* for uncountable nouns and *a few* for countable nouns.

I think the sauce needs a little more salt.
We need a few more chairs for the extra people.

> **Look!** We modify a superlative adjective using *one of*, *by far*, *easily*, or *nearly*.
> *She's one of the kindest people I've ever known.*
> *This is easily her best book in years.*

Modifying as (... as) comparisons

We modify *as* (... *as*) comparisons using *just*, *almost*, *nearly*, *half*, or *twice*. We express a small difference with *not quite* and a big one with *not nearly* or *nowhere near*.

You're just as smart as she is!
When we run, I'm nowhere near as fast as Jack. = Jack is much faster than I am.

Double comparatives

We also use the structure *the ... the ...* to make comparisons. The comparisons may include nouns, adjectives, adverbs, or entire clauses.

The less work I have, the happier I am.
The more excited she became, the louder she spoke.

Progressive comparatives

We can repeat a comparative adjective or adverb to emphasize that something is becoming increasingly hard/expensive/quick, etc.

It was getting harder and harder to breathe.
She's driving more and more dangerously.

GRAMMAR PRACTICE

1. Complete the sentences with the words in the box. You will need one word twice.

   > nowhere   easily   slightly   one   little   far
   > more   few   deal

   1. There's been a huge improvement in Sara's work this semester. It's been _____ better than last semester.
   2. It's certainly a good _____ hotter today than it was yesterday.
   3. It's getting more and _____ difficult to find somewhere to live in this city.
   4. Lucy and I are about the same weight. She's maybe _____ lighter than me.
   5. There were a _____ more guests at her last party.
   6. The mixture wasn't quite sweet enough, so I added a _____ more sugar.
   7. The cathedral is ancient – city hall is _____ near as old!
   8. We both agreed it was by _____ the most relaxing vacation we've ever had.
   9. Sam was a fantastic athlete. He was _____ the best athlete in his class.
   10. That was _____ of the worst meals I've ever eaten!

2. Complete the sentences with the correct form of the words in parentheses, plus any other words you need.

   1. It was terrible. It was _____ concert I've ever been to. (by far, bad)
   2. I wasn't so impressed with the pianist. She was _____ the violinist. (not nearly, skillful)
   3. This variety of the rose is _____ other varieties. (somewhat, pretty)
   4. It was _____ movies I've ever seen. (one of, good)
   5. Walking is _____ running. (nowhere near, tiring)
   6. I'm exhausted! That was _____ I've ever swum. (easily, far)
   7. The more you study, _____ . (easy, get)
   8. The cupcakes that they sell are _____ the ones you can make yourself. (just, good)

◀ Go back to page 27

99

GRAMMAR PRACTICE

4A Verb patterns (1): infinitives and -ing forms

 4.4

We **persuaded her to come** with us.
This **enabled me to spend** more time with my family.
She was **the youngest person to make** this trip alone.
I have **nothing to do**.
My mother **made me apologize** to him.
I **hate people being** rude to servers.
It's no use thinking about that now.

Infinitives

We use the infinitive with *to* after:

- some reporting verbs followed by an object, e.g., *advise, ask, beg, persuade, remind,* and *warn*.
  He begged her not to tell his parents.
- verbs expressing a preference + object such as *want, would like/hate,* and *prefer*.
  She'd like you to call her when you have a moment.
- verbs such as *allow, cause, enable,* and *force*.
  They were forced to sign the documents.
- indefinite pronouns such as *someone, something, anybody, everywhere*.
  I couldn't find anyone to help me with my homework.
- superlatives and expressions such as *the first, the next, the last, the only*.
  Jane was the only person to arrive on time.
- quantifiers and words expressing a degree such as *too, too much, too many, plenty of, too few,* and *not enough*.
  We didn't have enough time to fit everything in.

Infinitives vs. base forms

We use the base form after:

- the verbs *let, help,* and *make* + object.
  The teacher made him stand outside the classroom all morning.
  Could you help me move this table out of the way, please?
- after an object + *and, or, but, except,* and *than*.
  He's happy to do anything except study.
  She does nothing but complain. It drives me crazy!

-ing forms

We use the -ing form after:

- some verbs frequently followed by an object such as *love, hate, mind, stand, imagine, keep, remember, risk,* and *start*.
  Do you mind him interrupting you like that?
  I remembered him waving good-bye.
- expressions with *It* and *There's no*.
  There's no point spending loads of money on something you won't use.
  It's no use worrying about the problem and then doing nothing about it.
  It's pointless talking to him. He never listens.

Look! When an action is completed, we can use a perfect form:
I really regret having said what I did.

---

1 Complete the sentences with the correct form of the verbs in the box.

complete	drive	visit	complain
say	aim	call	make

1 Could you remind John _____ me?
2 Would you prefer me _____ now or later?
3 I remember Patrick _____ that he was an amazing cook.
4 We all need targets at work. They give us something _____ for.
5 It's no use _____ about the problem if you're not going to do anything to fix it!
6 The grant was fantastic because it enabled me _____ my studies.
7 The bumps in the road are supposed to discourage people from _____ too fast.
8 I can't stand people _____ noise when I'm trying to sleep.

2 Choose the correct options to complete the e-mail.

Hi Emily,

I just wanted to let you ¹*to know / know* that Jacob's doing OK, though obviously he's very upset about breaking up with Isabel. I've called him every day this week because I want him ²*knowing / to know* that I'm here for him if he needs me. I tried to persuade him ³*coming / to come* over tomorrow, but he says he's busy. I've invited him to several events recently, but, for now, I think he'd want us ⁴*to leave / leaving* him alone. I'm certainly going to stop calling him for a while. There's no point ⁵*to keep / keeping* on asking him if he's just not interested. I can't force him ⁶*be / to be* sociable if he doesn't want to! By the way, Jacob has asked me not ⁷*to tell / telling* Daniel.

Anyway, we should get together sometime soon! Why don't you let me ⁸*to cook / cook* dinner for you? Also, I've been decorating the apartment, and I'm really happy with it. I've done everything except ⁹*to paint / paint* the ceiling. You'll be the first person ¹⁰*seeing / to see* it!

Speak soon,

Love, Molly x

◀ Go back to page 31

4C Adding emphasis (2): inversion and do/does/did

▶ 4.12

Never had she known such sadness.
Rarely had I seen her so excited about anything.
Not only did we have a fantastic breakfast, **but** we also had a delicious dinner.
Not until I graduated **did I appreciate** my education.
The medicine didn't cure him completely, but it **did** help with the symptoms.
Isabel **does** want tickets for this Saturday after all.
Lionel **is** planning to come to our party.

Inversion after Never, Not until, etc.

We invert the subject and verb after some adverbial expressions when they begin a sentence. It is a way to add emphasis and tends to be slightly formal. In the simple present and simple past, we add the auxiliaries *do/does* and *did*.

I realized only then what a huge mistake I made. ⇨ *Only then did I realize what a huge mistake I made.*
We had hardly arrived when the phone rang. ⇨ *Hardly ever do we go out on weeknights.*

With some expressions we invert the subject and the verb in the first clause of the sentence. These expressions include *hardly (ever), in no way, little, never, not only, nowhere, only in this way, only later, only then, on no account, rarely, scarcely, seldom*, and *under no circumstances*.

Rarely have I been more excited by an exhibition.
Scarcely had she said the words than she regretted them.
Seldom had Sam experienced such kindness.
On no account had we agreed to that!

We also invert the subject and verb after the expressions *not only … but, hardly … than*, and *no sooner … than*.

Not only did he drive us to our hotel, but he also took our bags in for us.
No sooner had I given Sophie my umbrella than it started raining.

With some expressions we invert the subject and verb in the second clause of the sentence. These include *not since, not until, only after, only by + -ing, only now (that)*, and *only when*.

Not until I got home did it occur to me how stupid I'd been.
Only now (that) I'm older do I fully appreciate everything my parents did for me.

We can also use an *-ing* form after *not since, only after*, and *only when*.

Only when getting off the bus did we realize we'd gone in the wrong direction.

do/does/did in affirmative sentences

We sometimes use *do, does,* or *did* in affirmative sentences to emphasize the verb. Emphatic *do* is only used in affirmative, imperative, and simple past sentences.

She thought he wasn't coming, but he did eventually turn up.
Beth does help out with the cooking even if not very often.
I do love you. Really.
Do take your time to think things over.

In all other forms, the existing auxiliary is stressed for emphasis.

I have wished Tom a happy birthday!
I will pass this exam even if I have to study nonstop.

GRAMMAR PRACTICE

1 Complete the sentences with the words in the box.

| rarely | only | do | than | until | have |
| scarcely | sooner | was | did | | |

1 Not _____ I looked at the receipt did I realize how much we'd been charged.
2 Not only _____ he ten minutes late to the meeting, he also failed to bring his notes.
3 No _____ had I accepted the offer than I started to have doubts.
4 _____ had I sat down when there was a knock on the door.
5 She was pretty rude to us, but she _____ at least apologize to us later.
6 Seldom _____ I seen such a display of talent in such a young child.
7 James does most of the cooking, but I _____ make pizza now and then.
8 No sooner had we sat down on the beach _____ it started to rain!
9 Not _____ did they let us stay with them, they also showed us around the city.
10 _____ had I met anyone with such warmth and charm.

2 Put the words in the correct order to make sentences.

1 had / never before / cruelty / witnessed / he / such / terrible
   _____
2 had / woken up / I / no sooner / rang / the phone / when
   _____
3 didn't / did play / we / but / win / we / pretty well
   _____
4 did / that / only later / I reflect / had been / her behavior / quite bad
   _____
5 the hotel / not only / was also / room small / quite dirty / was / but it
   _____
6 his head / had / scarcely / the pillow / when he / touched / fell asleep
   _____
7 started raining / gotten my / no sooner / umbrella out / had I / than it
   _____
8 do like / I don't / but I / like jazz / blues
   _____

◀ Go back to page 35

GRAMMAR PRACTICE

5A Ellipsis and substitution

▶ 5.4

He came in **and** went straight to bed.
Sarah didn't go out, but we **did**.
I haven't told David, but maybe I **should**.
Joe thought that Oscar was mad, but he **wasn't**.
"So will the party be going ahead?" "I assume **so**."
"You're not going this evening, are you?" "I'm afraid **not**."

Ellipsis (omitting words)

After *and*, *but*, *or*, and *then*, we can omit the subject or the subject + auxiliary/modal verb. When the verb is the same, we can omit the entire verb.

She got in the car and she drove off.
We could eat out or we could order food in.

After auxiliaries and modals, we can omit the part of the sentence that is understood. The verb in the second clause may be different from the first clause.

I thought Max might pay for it, but apparently he won't pay for it.
We haven't eaten there, but perhaps we should eat there.
Mira doesn't eat fish, but I do eat fish.

We can also omit adjectives that are understood.

Tom was worried that he was rude to her, but he really wasn't rude.
Molly thinks she isn't smart, but she is smart.

Finally, we can also omit the same verb or verb phrase in a second clause when it follows an infinitive.

I asked Holly to go out with us this evening, but she didn't want to go out.
"Would you like to join us tonight?" "I'd love to join you tonight!"
"Should we invite Linda, too?" "Yes, I'd really like to invite Linda, too."

Substitution

We can substitute a countable noun with *one* if it is singular and *ones* if it is plural.

"Which coat is yours?" "It's the long, black one."
"Can you bring my sneakers, too?" "Which ones? The blue ones or the black ones?"

We can replace a negative clause with the word *not*.

"Are you going on vacation this summer?" "I'm afraid not."
Have you bought dinner? If not, I'll go to the supermarket now.
"Why isn't Jon here? Isn't he coming?" "I guess not."

We can replace a clause with the word *so*. *So* is common after verbs of supposition, such as *believe*, *expect*, *guess*, *hope*, *imagine*, *presume*, *suppose*, and *think*. We also use *so* after the verbs *afraid*, *appear*, *seem*, and *say*.

"Will Jamie be there?" "I expect so."
"Is the party still on tonight?" "I assume so, unless we hear otherwise."
"How do you know this dish has no peanuts?" "It says so."
"What? Dad's broken his leg?" "I'm afraid so."

> **Look!** After the verbs *believe*, *imagine*, and *think*, we usually replace a negative clause with a negative form of the auxiliary *do* and *so*.
> *"Does William play tennis?" "I don't think so."* NOT *"I think not."*
> *"They won't get here before dark, will they?" "I don't imagine so."*
> NOT *"I imagine not."*

1 Complete the sentences with the words in the box.

> should   to   haven't   one
> hope   don't   so (x2)   not (x2)

1 "Did Patrick pass his exam?" "I'm afraid _____."
2 "Do you think Michael was upset by her comment?" "I don't think _____."
3 "Would you like to play tennis with us?" "Yes, I'd love _____."
4 "Did Heather pass her exam?" "I imagine _____. She studied a lot."
5 Are you going to see Paul? If _____, I'll give him the message.
6 "Have you finished that essay, Hannah?" "No, I _____, I'm afraid."
7 I've never gone camping, but perhaps I _____.
8 "Will the trip be expensive?" "No, I _____ think so."
9 "If the problem continues, she'll have to close the restaurant." "I really _____ not."
10 "Which jacket did you buy in the end?" "The gray _____."

2 Match the two parts of the sentences.

1 She might refuse to help us, but I don't
2 Finn has been to Berlin, but I
3 I know I have to bring a coat for you, but I'm not sure
4 You could spend a lot on a flight there, but you really
5 I didn't like the movie at all, but both people I saw it with
6 Tom might be too sick to travel, but I
7 I haven't gone surfing, but I'd
8 She didn't come to the party even though she promised she

a haven't.   e would.
b shouldn't.   f which one.
c think so.   g hope not.
d love to.   h did.

3 Choose the correct options to complete the conversation.

A Is it cold out today?
B I imagine [1]*so / not*. Take a coat.
A But wasn't it supposed to be warmer?
B [2]*I hope not. / I'm afraid not*.
A But how do you know?
B The forecast said [3]*so / not*.
A Yeah, but it's been unreliable recently.
B I [4]*imagine / guess* so.
A It'll warm up for the weekend, though, right?
B I [5]*appear / presume* so.
A If it does, come to the beach with me.
B I'd absolutely love [6]*to / so*.

102

◀ Go back to page 41

5C Noun phrases

 5.8

I lived in the apartment **next to the park**.
Jack was the guy **waving from the other side of the street**.
We have a proposal **to make driving safer**.
These are some ideas **that I thought of yesterday**.
He gave me **a beautiful blue sugar bowl**.

Information after the noun

A noun phrase consists of a noun + other information, which can include phrases with prepositions, -ing forms, infinitives, and clauses.

I preferred the pants *in the first store we went to*.
We saw the woman *watching us as we locked our door*.
We have tickets *to go to a Shakira concert with Andy*.
Was that the woman *who sold you the bike*?

Information before the noun

Information before a noun can include determiners, articles, adjectives, and adverbs.

Those earrings are really beautiful.
A river runs through the center of town.
It was a *thoroughly unpleasant* experience.
That *beautifully written* book brought tears to my eyes!

When we use more than one adjective before a noun, opinion words usually come before factual words, and we use the following order for other adjectives:
size + shape + age + color + origin + material + purpose.

She was wearing a gorgeous yellow dress.
It's a big square metal box for keeping coins in.
Delicious freshly baked chocolate brownies are my weakness!

> **Look!** Using noun phrases helps us express ourselves more concisely. We may give several pieces of information in a noun phrase, both before and after the noun that we are describing:
> I read *an absolutely fascinating* article *in that magazine that James left behind*.

With possessive 's or of

The possessive *'s* and *of* express the general idea of "having" that links two nouns. We usually use *'s* for people, and a phrase with *of* for things and abstract nouns. We also usually use *of* to express possession in long phrases.

I never actually saw *his parents'* house.
She's the daughter *of the woman who was arrested for robbery*.

With plural nouns the apostrophe follows the *s*, but with irregular plurals (*women, men, people, children*) we use *'s*.

The rugby players' shorts were filthy.
People's opinions matter.

Noun + noun compounds

Noun + noun compounds usually have a more specific meaning than the two separate nouns. The first noun is always singular, and describes the second noun.

I'd like to stop at the *guitar store*.
He watches all the *comedy shows*.

GRAMMAR PRACTICE

1 Choose the correct options to complete the sentences.
 1 We have plans *to go / going* to Paris next year.
 2 Was that our *cowboy boots' neighbor / neighbor with the cowboy boots*?
 3 The *chair's leg / leg of the chair* just fell off!
 4 It was a *truly horrifying experience / horrifying experience truly*.
 5 Do you need *a can opener / an opener of cans*?
 6 She's the *sister of the mayor in the next town / mayor in the next town's sister*.
 7 She has *an incredible talent for remembering everything she learns / a talent for incredibly remembering everything she learns*.
 8 I think I'm going to buy a *ceiling fan / fan ceiling*.
 9 Have you seen *a child's blue sweater / a blue sweater of a child* anywhere?
 10 I think that man might be *Norwegian Airlines's CEO / the CEO of Norwegian Airlines*.

2 Rewrite the sentences with the adjectives in the correct order.

 1 We've bought a [gray / wool / long] sofa.
 _____
 2 She lived in a [little / stone / pretty] cottage.
 _____
 3 He introduced me to a [Turkish / elderly / very nice] woman.
 _____
 4 We ate some [French / delicious / chocolate] cookies.
 _____
 5 I noticed she was wearing a [small / nice / silver] watch.
 _____
 6 He was with a [Swedish / slender / tall] woman.
 _____
 7 What's the name of that [dark-haired / short / Irish] actor?
 _____
 8 I remember they had a [wooden / old / beautiful] table.
 _____

◀ Go back to page 45

VOCABULARY PRACTICE

1A Attitudes and emotions

1 ▶ 1.1 Match verbs 1–6 with definitions a–f. Then match idioms 7–12 with definitions g–l. Listen and check.

1 throw yourself into (something)
2 cheer up
3 feel down
4 get carried away
5 come across as
6 get into (something)

a appear to have a certain characteristic
b get excited or feel too much emotion
c be depressed or unhappy
d quickly and enthusiastically start a task
e develop a new hobby or interest
f become (or make someone) happier when sad

7 be over the moon
8 look on the bright side
9 be on the ball
10 keep your cool
11 be green with envy
12 be down to earth

g stay calm in dangerous or emotional situations
h have a positive approach to life
i be practical, sensible, and friendly
j feel very jealous
k be quick to respond to new ideas and information
l feel extremely happy

2 Complete the sentences with a form of a verb or idiom from exercise 1.

1 During his speech the best man _____ and talked for over an hour.
2 My neighbor's really nice, not at all like her husband, who's a little pretentious. She's very _____ .
3 Stock market traders have to _____ the whole time – quick to react to changes in the market and make decisions.
4 Even when life gets really tough, my mom always _____ . She's never negative.
5 My new boss _____ being really impatient, but, actually, she's not.
6 James tends to _____ a project without thinking. He needs to plan ahead more.
7 I've never seen her panic. She always manages to _____ .
8 I was _____ with my test grades – I got all "A"s!
9 When Irina moved to a new city, she _____ and really lonely since she didn't know anyone.
10 Ian had been feeling a little down, but he _____ when his girlfriend called.
11 Our next-door neighbors bought a Porsche. My husband wants one – he's _____ .
12 I slowly _____ playing the guitar after a friend taught me a few chords, and now I'm in a band.

3 ▶ 1.2 Match adjectives 1–7 with definitions a–g. Listen and check.

1 open-minded
2 courageous
3 conscientious
4 sarcastic
5 astonished
6 thankful
7 disgusted

a very surprised
b pleased, grateful, and relieved
c brave or unafraid
d feeling strong unhappiness or disapproval
e willing to consider new ideas
f hard-working and thorough
g ironic, often when being critical

4 Complete the sentences with an adjective from exercise 3.

1 I was _____ that my teenage brother had cleaned his room without being asked to!
2 The instructors were very _____ during the course. They took notes, gave feedback, and helped all the students as much as possible.
3 Being _____ is about actively overcoming your fears.
4 He said my haircut was "amazing," but he sounded a little _____ .
5 We're _____ the weather is getting better because we're going to the beach tomorrow.
6 He was _____ to read about several robberies in his area in the news.
7 My manager is very _____ and listens to everyone's opinion before she makes a decision.

◀ Go back to page 4

VOCABULARY PRACTICE

1C Abstract nouns

1 ▶ 1.7 Make nouns from the words in the box below and write them in the correct column of the chart. Listen and check.

| annoy | inconvenient | aware | kind | bored | member | curious | relation | hate | reliable | honest | wise |

-ity	-ness	-ship
sensitivity generosity	fairness selfishness	friendship leadership

-ance / -ence	-dom	others
tolerance patience	freedom kingdom	pride loyalty

2 Complete the sentences. Use abstract nouns for the verbs or adjectives in **bold**.

1 Bill is **annoyed** because he is short of money. It's obvious.
   Bill's _____ because he is short of money is obvious.
2 My roommate **hates** pets, which is surprising. It's **selfish** and it bothers me.
   My roomate's _____ of pets is surprising. Her _____ bothers me.
3 My boyfriend was so **sensitive** when I lost my job. It was wonderful.
   My boyfriend's _____ when I lost my job was wonderful.
4 A good boss is **reliable**, **fair**, and **patient**.
   A good boss displays _____ , _____ , and _____ .
5 Open-minded people are **aware** and **tolerant**.
   Open-minded people show _____ and _____ .

3 Complete the text with abstract nouns from the chart in exercise 1.

Southam University

Life in college: read what one of our new students has to say

I love my new life as a student! I have a good ¹_____ with all my teachers, and I take ²_____ in my work. And can you believe I've signed up for a ³_____ course? I'm hoping to become a manager some day.

I've met lots of new people, and I'm now sharing an apartment with someone I've developed a close ⁴_____ with. While it's pretty far from school, the ⁵_____ of living off-campus is balanced by the ⁶_____ of living in my own place – I can do what I want whenever I feel like it. ⁷_____ used to be a problem I had at my parents' home since there wasn't much to do in the area, but now I spend my time exploring my new neighborhood.

I admit things are a little tight financially. The ⁸_____ fee for the local sports club was way beyond my budget. But the ⁹_____ of others amazes me. A neighbor offered to pay the fee for me!

◀ Go back to page 8

VOCABULARY PRACTICE

2A Health and medical treatment

1 ▶ 2.1 Match words 1–10 with pictures a–j. Listen and check.

1 bruise ____   6 kidneys ____
2 lungs ____   7 liver ____
3 Band-Aid ____   8 blister ____
4 bandage ____   9 ribs ____
5 spine ____   10 cast ____

2 Complete the sentences with words from the box. Use each item once.

| heart disease   high blood pressure   injection   scan   side effects |
| splitting headache   stitches   upset stomach   X-ray |

1 I try to avoid salt in my diet because I have _____ .
2 He had an _____ at the hospital and discovered that he'd broken his wrist.
3 My sister cut her hand pretty badly and had to have _____ .
4 The doctor says I can have an _____ in my knee to reduce the swelling.
5 Some people don't even know they have _____ until they have chest pain.
6 I once had an _____ after eating in that restaurant, and I haven't been back since.
7 I'm going to take a pill – I have a _____ from all this noise.
8 Some people taking the medicine have _____ , including headaches, mild fever, and problems sleeping.
9 He had a brain _____ after his fall to check that there was no damage.

3 ▶ 2.2 Read sentences 1–7. Match the words and phrases in **bold** with definitions a–g. Listen and check.

1 If you don't warm up properly before you exercise, you can **pull a muscle**.
2 I thought if I jumped and landed badly, I might **sprain** my ankle.
3 If you work closely with other people in an office, it's very easy to **pick up a bug**.
4 You might have to **take antibiotics** to get rid of the infection.
5 If my grandma stands up too quickly, she can **feel dizzy**.
6 My sister can't eat nuts because she's **allergic** to them.
7 My doctor has arranged for me to **see a specialist** about my foot problem.

a have a meeting with a doctor who is an expert in one particular medical problem
b have a sudden reaction and become sick if you eat, touch, or breathe a particular substance
c stretch and injure an organ surrounded by soft tissue that produces movement
d feel that you might fall because everything around you seems to be moving
e get some type of sickness from a place or another person
f take a medicine that kills bacteria in the body and, therefore, cures sickness
g injure a hand, wrist, or ankle by twisting it or moving it suddenly

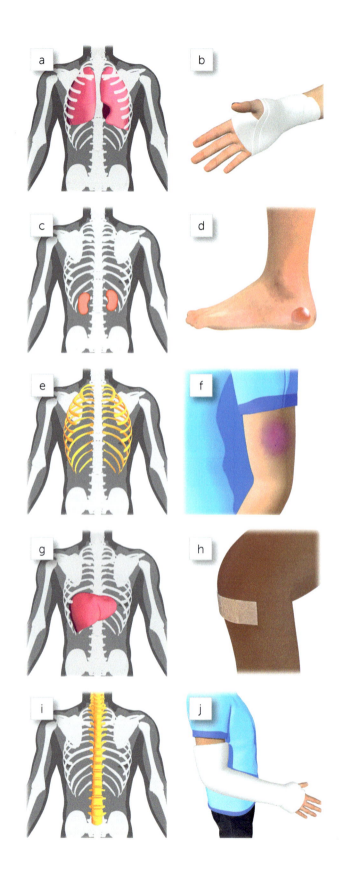

◀ Go back to page 12

VOCABULARY PRACTICE

2B Life skills and well-being

1 ▶ 2.7 Match the **bold** words and phrases 1–6 with definitions a–f. Then match 7–11 with definitions g–k. Listen and check.

  1 I wanted to stop my driving lessons, but my friend encouraged me to **persevere** with them. _____

  2 I'm going to ask two other artists to **collaborate** with me on an exhibit. _____

  3 Some people are good at **handling** stressful situations, but others get very stressed. _____

  4 I try to **manage** my stress by playing a lot of sports. _____

  5 You need to **prioritize** your **workload** so that you meet all your deadlines. _____

  6 The intern has **shown initiative** identifying problems in our computer system and fixing them. _____

  7 Governments should **cooperate** more with each other to ensure peace. _____

  8 Every year I **set goals** for myself, like trying a new sport or eating healthier food. _____

  9 If you have a problem, it's better to **deal with** it rather than ignore it. _____

  10 There was so much pressure at work that we found it hard to **cope**. _____

  11 I decided to **take the initiative** and start a meditation group at work. _____

  a work with others on a project or toward the same goal
  b continue doing something, even though it's difficult
  c decide which tasks are the most important and do them first
  d take action or respond successfully to a difficult feeling or situation
  e develop strategies to be on top of something difficult
  f demonstrate a willingness to get things done and take responsibility

  g take the first action in a situation
  h create aims
  i work with others in a helpful and communicative way
  j develop a way to address a problem
  k successfully navigate a difficult situation

◀ Go back to page 14

2C Verbs and nouns with the same form

1 ▶ 2.10 Complete each pair of sentences with the correct form of the words in the box. Listen and check.

balance   concern   envy   harm   panic   regret

  1 a It _____ me that, at twenty-two, she's never had a job. I find it worrying.
     b I'm afraid I have a number of _____ relating to his health.

  2 a I really _____ not having spent more time with my grandparents when I was younger.
     b My biggest _____ is that I never learned another language.

  3 a I've always _____ people who have the confidence to speak in public. I find it impossible.
     b I watched with _____ as Lara and Sophie drove off to the beach.

  4 a I have a full-time job and two small children. It's a struggle to _____ my work and family commitments.
     b There are too few female politicians. We need a better gender _____ .

  5 a There was a loud bang, and _____ quickly spread through the crowd.
     b I suddenly noticed that my bag was gone, and I _____ .

  6 a As a public figure, he didn't want the facts to become known in case it _____ his reputation.
     b A bad night's sleep once in a while won't do you any _____ .

2 ▶ 2.11 Rewrite the sentences, replacing the underlined words with the verb form of the noun. Make any other necessary changes.

  1 The earthquakes <u>have had a negative impact</u> on the economy.
     The earthquakes have impacted the economy negatively.

  2 Could you <u>give me an update</u> on how the project is going?
     _____

  3 The prisoners <u>made their escape</u> by digging a tunnel.
     _____

  4 Top tennis players <u>make a lot of sacrifices</u> for their careers.
     _____

  5 She studied hard and <u>kept her focus</u> on passing her exams.
     _____

  6 Living in a small town <u>has great benefits</u> for older people.
     _____

◀ Go back to page 16

117

VOCABULARY PRACTICE

3A Change and time

1 ▶ 3.1 Match words and phrases in **bold** 1–12 with definitions a–l. Listen and check.
   1 It's not a modern movie – it's set in the post-war **era**.
   2 This was a style that was fashionable at the **turn of the century**.
   3 The task requires you to put various inventions **in chronological order**.
   4 I've given up eating meat and fish **for good**.
   5 A **leap year** occurs every four years.
   6 Some of the world's exotic animals will soon **die out**.
   7 When Emma's clothes **go out of fashion**, she stops wearing them.
   8 Tim decided to **switch** from glasses to contact lenses.
   9 We need to **modify** the website to make it easier to navigate.
   10 I could scarcely recognize the city. It had undergone a total **transformation**.
   11 Although property prices have gone up, they will probably **stabilize** soon.
   12 When I lost my job, I had to **make a major adjustment** to my lifestyle.

   a adapt or become used to a very different situation
   b stop changing; become firmly established
   c make partial changes to something
   d a long period of history
   e one that has an extra day in February
   f change from something to; exchange something for something else
   g the beginning of a period of 100 years
   h put events one after the other, based on when they happened
   i end; become completely extinct
   j become unpopular; no longer considered smart or stylish
   k a very noticeable change in form, nature, or appearance
   l forever; definitively

Time flies when you're having fun

2 ▶ 3.2 Complete the text with words and phrases from the box. Listen and check.

   | adapt to | become obsolete | decade | evolve | for the time being |
   | in those days | in the long term | in your lifetime | millennium | transition |

My birthday's coming, and I'm approaching the big two-oh! For many people, this ¹_____ is the ten years when big things happen! ²_____ I'm in college, but in a few years, I'll have finished my education, and I'll get a job. I may even find my life partner. (Just as an aside, my own parents got married at 19! ³_____, that was common.) Anyway, an online life coach describes our twenties as "the period in which our characters ⁴_____, and we make the ⁵_____ to adulthood." That's a lot of change ahead! Yet haven't you seen a lot of change already ⁶_____? Since the start of the ⁷_____, just after I was born, there has been huge technological change. Even the phone I bought two years ago is old and has almost ⁸_____. We're a flexible generation. We can ⁹_____ anything. Still, I can't help wondering what I'll be doing in ten years. I guess ¹⁰_____, it will become clear!

◀ Go back to page 22

VOCABULARY PRACTICE

3C Expressions with *come* and *go*

1 ▶ 3.7 Match sentences 1–8 with pictures a–h. Listen and check.
   1 We've been discussing this issue for hours without finding a solution. We're just **going around in circles**. ____
   2 Oscar felt guilty about having a new girlfriend and decided to **come clean**. ____
   3 We won't have lunch for two or three hours. Here, have this to **keep you going**. ____
   4 For Angela, work always **comes first**. ____
   5 Wow, what a busy day! I've **been on the go** since dawn. ____
   6 Something is always **going wrong** with this PC! ____
   7 Our neighbor James told us about his vacation plans, but he didn't **go into detail**. ____
   8 We've done well this month, but we still **have a long way to go** to reach our target. ____

2 ▶ 3.8 Replace the underlined phrases with the correct form of a phrase in the box. Listen and check.

> come to light   come easily   come up   come up against   go according to plan   go from strength to strength
> go missing   how come   it goes without saying   still / yet to come   when it comes to

   1 It's been a really difficult project from start to finish. We've <u>had to deal with</u> so many problems.
   2 Jack studies hard in class, but, <u>when the situation involves</u> homework, he's incredibly lazy.
   3 <u>It is very obvious</u> that children need encouragement from their teachers.
   4 I'm sure everything will <u>happen in the way that is wanted</u>, and the party will be a huge success.
   5 Evidence may yet <u>be discovered</u> which proves us wrong.
   6 We've made three payments, but the biggest bill is <u>expected soon</u>.
   7 <u>What is the reason</u> you are home so early? I thought you were working late tonight.
   8 Ellen has never struggled with math or science and says they really <u>take no effort</u>.
   9 He already had two successful restaurants, and now he's opened a third. He's <u>becoming more and more successful</u>.
   10 When people <u>disappear, or seem to disappear</u>, their pictures are often posted on social media.
   11 I'm sure I'll be at the party unless something <u>happens that I wasn't expecting</u>.

◀ Go back to page 26

VOCABULARY PRACTICE

4A Success and failure

1 ▶ 4.2 Read the text. Match the phrases in **bold** 1–10 with definitions a–j. Listen and check.

Success has always come easily to my brother. He [1] **thrived** at school, [2] **passing with flying colors** and then he got a degree from a top-rate university. When he told the family he was setting up a business to sell a new children's toy he'd invented, we all knew he'd make a success of it. And sure enough, within a year, his product had [3] **caught on**, and he'd [4] **met** the ambitious **targets** that he'd set himself financially.

And what was I up to all this time? I was [5] **failing miserably** at everything. Or so I thought. Was I [6] **messing up** on my studies or [7] **falling short** of my expectations at work? No, I was working hard and never [8] **missed a deadline**. The truth is, I was failing in my head. I was comparing myself with my brother and, as a consequence, nothing that I [9] **accomplished** was ever enough. It was this feeling of not being as good that was [10] **holding me back**.

a keep someone from getting ahead or developing
b become known/popular (an item, trend, etc.)
c achieve; be successful at a task
d be not just a little unsuccessful, but extremely unsuccessful
e do well and prosper in general
f get a very high grade on a test
g fail to do something by the necessary date
h achieve a specific objective decided in advance
i make mistakes; spoil things
j complete something, but not manage to meet a required goal

2 ▶ 4.3 Complete the expressions in **bold** with the words in the box. Listen and check.

ambition   balloon   blame   fell   go   expectations   lacking   made   success   triumph

1 So the question is, who **was to** _____ for this terrible war?
2 He never really _____ **it** as an actor and, instead, earned a living doing a variety of jobs.
3 The course itself was fantastic, far **exceeding** my _____ .
4 Kumar was very motivated. After years of training, he was finally able to **fulfill** his _____ to become a doctor.
5 Her skincare company did well. Indeed, it was one of the _____ **stories** of the decade.
6 Yes, there were difficulties, but Taylor managed to _____ **over** them and build a hugely successful brand.
7 My attempt to tell an amusing story on the subject _____ **flat**. Nobody laughed – not one person!
8 So how does a multimillion dollar company _____ **bankrupt**?
9 They clearly didn't like my suggestion. It **went over like a lead** _____ !
10 He's very practical, but he's totally _____ **in** imagination.

◀ Go back to page 30

4B Expressions with *make* and *take*

1 ▶ 4.6 Complete the expressions in **bold** with the correct form of *make* or *take*. Listen and check.

1 I need to _____ more **time** for my family because I have such a full schedule at work.
2 I asked the salesclerk if she could hurry up as I had a train to catch. She _____ **it the wrong way** and was pretty offended.
3 Because Ana's rent's gone up, she's taken a second job in order to _____ **ends meet**.
4 It really _____ Daniel's **day** to hear that he'd been accepted into law school!
5 Adam's girlfriend's broken up with him. I thought he would _____ **it well**, but he's actually _____ **it** really **badly**.
6 Molly was very sick a few years ago, so she never _____ her health **for granted** now.
7 I don't recognize this street. Do you think we've _____ **a wrong turn**?
8 We'd planned to go to the beach this weekend, but rain was forecast. We decided to _____ **a chance** and go anyway.
9 I bought tickets for my brother's favorite band to _____ **it up to** him for damaging his car.
10 Our week away didn't start well because our flight was canceled, but we _____ **the best of** the situation and had a great week at home.
11 My grandmother always tells me to _____ **the most of** my youth, as it doesn't last forever.

120

◀ Go back to page 32

VOCABULARY PRACTICE

4C Idioms

1 ▶ 4.10 Match the idioms in **bold** 1–8 with definitions a–h. Listen and check.

I have a new job! I'd been unhappy at work for a while. Basically, one of my colleagues was incredibly lazy and for over a year, I'd been doing her work, as well as my own. For some reason, my boss just ¹ **turned a blind eye** to the problem. In March, I was asked to take on another project, and it ² **was the last straw**. I decided to ³ **call it a day**, and the very next day I resigned. Anyway, during my last week at work and completely ⁴ **out of the blue**, an ex-colleague got in touch. To make a long story short, she asked me to come and set up the design software at her company since I ⁵ **know it inside out**! I work in the office three days a week (the other two at home), so it's ⁶ **the best of both worlds**, really. The commute to work is a lot further – the train fare ⁷ **costs an arm and a leg**! – but I'm happy. So, a tough start to the year, but I guess it was all ⁸ **a blessing in disguise**!

a decide or agree to stop doing something
b with no warning that something would happen
c be very expensive
d something that seems bad when it happens, but that brings benefits later
e a situation where you get the benefits of two very different things
f have a lot of knowledge of a subject
g ignore something bad so you don't have to deal with it
h a problem, after many other problems, which makes you finally take action

2 ▶ 4.11 Match the underlined part of sentences 1–8 with idioms a–h. Listen and check.

1 You'll have no trouble passing the exam, Olivia. I took it last month, and it's <u>really easy</u>!
2 If I were you, I wouldn't add any more projects this year. You don't want to <u>take on too much work</u>.
3 There's the question of how you actually pay for the service once it's set up, but you can <u>deal with that problem when it happens</u>.
4 That was a fascinating talk, Daniel. You've certainly given us plenty of <u>ideas to think about</u>.
5 Millie's not going to change her mind on this. My suggestion is not to <u>try to do something that is impossible</u> here.
6 After working so hard for so long, it's nice to be able to <u>relax and enjoy yourself without worrying what people think</u>.
7 I think you're absolutely right about Anna being jealous. You've <u>described the true cause of the problem</u>.
8 Amy doesn't really own a castle – she just loves to <u>joke by telling you something false</u>!

a hit the nail on the head
b let your hair down
c cross that bridge when you come to it
d pull your leg
e fight a losing battle
f food for thought
g a piece of cake
h bite off more than you can chew

3 Write captions for pictures 1–4 using the idioms.

1 These sneakers _____ .
2 I know this topic _____ .
3 It looks hard. Actually, _____ .
4 I think Grandpa was _____ .

◀ Go back to page 34

121

VOCABULARY PRACTICE

5A Tastes and opinions

1 ▶ 5.1 Complete the conversation with the words in the box. Listen and check.

> adores appalling appeal desire despise fabulous face fan inadequate mediocre

A So what was the food like when you were away?
B A little disappointing, to be honest. It was fairly ¹_____ – you know, just not very good, and a little overpriced.
A I know what you mean. I have no ²_____ to spend all my money on bad food.
B One meal that sticks in my mind was ³_____ – not only was the food completely cold, but the waiter was rude, too. I really can't ⁴_____ even one more rude waiter.
A I know what you mean! I really ⁵_____ bad service!
B Actually, we did have some good seafood on our last night. I'm not a huge ⁶_____ of fish – it doesn't really ⁷_____ to me – but my friend ⁸_____ it, and she'd heard there was a ⁹_____ seafood restaurant nearby.
A That's great. At least your last night was memorable.
B Yes, but the amount of food was ¹⁰_____ . The appetizer was one tiny shrimp!

2 Match the words and phrases that have a similar meaning.

1 detest	**a** not be wild about
2 just average	**b** sensational
3 not be a huge fan of	**c** exceptional
4 spectacular	**d** mediocre
5 outstanding	**e** despise

3 ▶ 5.2 Match the <u>underlined</u> part of sentences 1–10 with a–j. Listen and check.

1 The show isn't great. I don't know why everyone <u>loves it so much</u>.
2 Klara loves that singer. She's <u>always thinking and talking about</u> him.
3 I'm not crazy about camping, but I <u>think it's better than</u> a cheap hotel.
4 If I'm honest, I found the movie <u>somewhat boring and too long</u>.
5 The products sold in that store are <u>low quality</u>.
6 She talks all the time, and it really <u>irritates me</u>!
7 It was a fantastic show – really <u>exciting and impressive</u>.
8 I've seen the trailer for the movie and it looks <u>likely to be good</u>.
9 Molly is so impatient – she <u>hates</u> waiting for anything.
10 I'll come shopping with you if you'd like, but I don't <u>really want to</u> go.

a promising
b gets on my nerves
c have a strong desire to
d detests
e inferior
f tedious
g obsessed with
h is wild about it
i find it preferable to
j sensational

◀ Go back to page 40

5C Verb suffixes

1 ▶ 5.7 Make verbs from the words in the box below and write them in the correct column of the chart. Listen and check.

> anticipation association bright clarification deterioration
> emphasis exaggeration generalization justification
> minimization negotiation notification ripe simplification
> soft specification straight summary sweet sympathy
> weak

-ate	-en	-ize	-ify
exaggerate	*straighten*	*generalize*	*justify*

2 Choose the correct options to complete the sentences.

1 Her hair is naturally curly, but she *straightens / brightens* it every day.
2 After much discussion, a deal has been *exaggerated / negotiated*.
3 The cereal is sugar-free, but you can *sweeten / soften* it if you like.
4 Let the grapefruit *weaken / ripen* before eating it.
5 After walking uphill, I could feel my legs starting to *soften / weaken*.
6 It wasn't that bad, María! You're *deteriorating / exaggerating*!
7 She *summarized / generalized* the talk in sixty seconds.
8 After missing the meeting, she tried to *justify / sympathize* her absence.

◀ Go back to page 44

COMMUNICATION PRACTICE

1A Student A

1 Look at the picture and read the story behind it.

- Scientists consider the happiest man in the world to be Matthieu Ricard, a Buddhist monk.
- After completing his doctoral thesis in genetics in 1972, he gave up his scientific career. He's been studying Tibetan Buddhism ever since.
- He's taken part in research that shows that people who have meditated for over 10,000 hours experience a high level of positive emotions.
- He believes that people who are constantly trying to be content actually end up feeling miserable, and he also thinks that happiness is a skill we need to work hard at to master.
- He says that things still annoy him, but he quickly starts laughing at them and lets them go.

2 Cover the text and tell Student B the story behind your picture.

3 Look at Student B's picture and listen to the story behind it.

1C Student A

1 Read your sentences and listen to Student B's responses.

1	A	Frank went to the movies with Sarah.
	B	…
2	A	I'm really worried about the economy.
	B	…
3	A	Tina went to the wrong room for the meeting.
	B	…
4	A	You need a good rest.
	B	…

2 Listen to Student B's sentences and respond using the prompts.

1	B	…
	A	No. it was Sandra …
2	B	…
	A	Really? The place …
3	B	…
	A	No, what happened was …
4	B	…
	A	Really? It was my …

130

COMMUNICATION PRACTICE

1D Student A

1 Student B will give you a topic to talk about.

2 Talk about the topic for one minute without stopping. Use paraphrasing to emphasize and clarify, and fillers to avoid long pauses.

3 Choose one of the topics below for Student B to talk about for one minute.
How many types of fillers does he/she use?

- the type of movies you like
- your favorite and least favorite subjects in school

2A Student A

1 Read Alex's description of veganism.

Being Vegan

I've been a vegan for a year now, and I've never felt better! Vegans don't eat or use any animal products at all, so that includes things like milk, eggs, and even honey and wool. A vegan diet is healthy, but you do have to make sure you eat a wide range of foods. For example, apricots and green vegetables are full of iron and will stop you from feeling dizzy. Also, you probably won't pick up as many bugs because of all the vitamins you get from fruit and vegetables. The only thing that doesn't occur naturally in plants is vitamin B12, which is important for the health of your spine, so it's essential to take B12 supplements.

2 Cover the text. Tell Student B about veganism, using the prompts below.
- Vegans aren't supposed to ...
- If you're a vegan, you need to ...
- One of the advantages of being vegan is that you're less likely to ...
- To keep your spine healthy, you have to ...

3 Listen to Student B talking about hot yoga. Would you like to try it?

COMMUNICATION PRACTICE

2C Student A

1 Use the information in the box to tell Student B about Matt, a friend who has upset you. Add some details to your story to make it more realistic. Student B will respond after each point.

> 1 You'd had plans to meet your friend Matt for lunch, but he didn't show up. He didn't even call to cancel at the last minute, and you had to eat alone. You were so angry you blocked him on all your social media accounts.
>
> 2 It's not the first time he's done this. It's happened on several occasions. The last time, you patiently explained that if you had known he wasn't going to come, you could have planned to do something else. He apologized profusely and promised that he'd never do it again.
>
> 3 You don't know whether you should bother making an effort to be friends with him any more.

2 Student B will tell you three things about something that happened with his/her friend Pilar. Respond after each point. Use the prompts a–c.

> a It probably has nothing to do with you. She could be … She might not have had …
> b Maybe you just caught her at a bad moment. She may have been … or she could have had …
> c She may have a real problem you don't know about. You shouldn't have been … You could have … What you said must have really …

3A Student A

1 Look at the picture and read the story behind it.

2 Cover the text and tell Student B the story behind your picture.

3 Look at Student B's picture and listen to the story behind it.

After a wonderful vacation in New York, Shoshana and her partner Dez were devastated to discover that they had lost the memory card for their camera. They put a message on the lost-and-found section of a major website, but with no luck. Every now and then, they would think sadly about the lost photos, but after a while, they accepted that the card had disappeared for good.

However, three years later, they received a letter – containing the memory card! A member of the staff at the Museum of Modern Art had been working on the day that Shoshana and Dez had visited and had noticed it lying on the floor. She posted the photos on a site called "ifoundyourcamera.net." Luckily for Shoshana, the daughter of one of her friends was looking at that site one day when she was bored. She saw the photos. She was amazed to recognize her mom's friend, and delighted to be able to arrange for the card to be returned to Shoshana.

COMMUNICATION PRACTICE

3C Student A

1 Read the takeout pizza menu.

Takeout Menu
Pizzas

The Monster Meat   **$16.99**
With heaps of ham, pepperoni, ground beef, and sausage on a thick layer of creamy melted mozzarella cheese and our famous tomato sauce, this one is the carnivore's dream! (1,300 calories)

The Slimmer's Friend   **$11.99**
This delicious, yet healthy, pizza has a hole in the middle that is filled with salad and a low-fat honey and mustard dressing. Topped with peppers, mushrooms, and spinach, there's a little less cheese than usual, but the same creamy taste. (Vegetarian; 440 calories)

The Smokin' Hot   **$13.99**
A generous scattering of finely chopped chilis turns this pepperoni pizza into a taste explosion! Served on an extra large crispy base, with fresh tomatoes and plenty of mozzarella. (880 calories)

2 Tell Student B about the three pizzas. Then answer Student B's questions. Use some of the expressions in the box.

> nowhere near as   by far the   far more   significantly less
> twice as   a good deal   not quite as   one of the

3 Listen to Student B tell you about three desserts on his/her takeout menu. Ask questions about the desserts with the words and phrases in the box. Decide which dessert you want.

> largest   healthiest   sweetest   most economical
> most fattening   tastiest

3D Students A and B

1 Take turns fixing the information in **bold** with the information in the box. Use *you know* or *I mean*.

1 So we were **about to get up in front of the whole class** to give our presentation when Jen looked down and realized she'd put on one blue boot and one black boot.
   ERROR: we'd just gotten up in front of the whole class.

2 My friend invited me to a party, and **I didn't really …** But she persuaded me to come, and I met someone who is now my boyfriend. We've been together for three years!
   REFORMULATE: I'd had a long day studying, and I was tired.

3 My aunt **wasn't …** and when my boss found out, he told me to take a few days off. Not many bosses would do that. It was really kind.
   REFORMULATE: She had to have emergency heart surgery.

4 I went to see my favorite band play at the stadium. I was near the front, and halfway through the concert, **the lead singer** threw his jacket into the crowd. And I caught it!
   ERROR: the piano player

5 I went to a midnight show of a horror movie once. My girlfriend suggested it, and I wasn't scared. But **it was absolutely terrifying**!
   FALSE START: it was absolutely

6 I was lining up at a fast food restaurant in another town, thousands of miles from home. **Suddenly I noticed** the guy in front of me was my best friend from high school. I hadn't seen him in years!
   FALSE START: I noticed

133

COMMUNICATION PRACTICE

4A Student A

1 Tell Student B about the problem your friend Andy is having. Use the information in the box.

> Andy wants to be a rock guitarist, but the idea has gone over like a lead balloon with his parents, who want him to become a doctor. He's started medical school, but he's unhappy there. He respects his parents and doesn't want to upset them, but he feels they're holding him back from fulfilling his dream. He knows that being a musician is a risky career choice, but he really loves playing the guitar.

2 Listen to Student B's advice. Respond by saying whether or not you think it is good advice, or by asking for further explanation, if necessary.

3 Listen to Student B telling you about the problem his/her friend Lucy is having.

4 Choose six of the phrases in the box to give Student B some advice: three for things he/she should do and three for things he/she shouldn't do to help Lucy.

| persuade her   warn her   help her   remind her
| There's no point   It might be a good idea   encourage her |

4C Student A

1 Read the statements. Discuss whether you think they are true.

- Never before have people been so obsessed with how they look.
- Not unless you have been homeless yourself can you really understand how difficult it is.
- Only after knowing someone for at least two years should you consider marrying them.
- No sooner do you buy a new phone than a new and better one becomes available.

2 Listen to Student B's statements. Discuss whether you think they are true.

5A Student A

1 Ask Student B questions 1–5. Listen to his/her answers.
   1 Are you going to replace your phone with a newer one sometime soon? If so, can I come phone shopping with you?
   2 Have you seen Carl recently? I've called him but there's no answer. Should we ask him to go out with us this weekend?
   3 Did you hear? Ana has gotten married to that guy she met when she was living in Sydney and working at the art gallery!
   4 I know you love chocolate cake, so I got you one for your birthday – do you like it?
   5 Have you been to the Italian restaurant or the Chinese place? If not, should we go to one of them?

2 Listen to Student B's questions. Choose the correct response a–e.
   a I know that Jamie does, but I don't think Tara's wild about it. She might enjoy a mild one, though.
   b The supermarket sells them, and so does the grocer on the corner. Or you can get them at the market if you prefer to.
   c I'll do it if you're desperate, but I'd prefer not to because the traffic's always horrible. It would be quicker to take a train if you can.
   d I could, but I'd rather not. I can stay late tonight, though, if you'd like me to.
   e My friend Max does. I can ask him, if you'd like, or just give you his phone number, and you can call him yourself if you want to.

134

COMMUNICATION PRACTICE

5C Student A

1 Read the first part of the article to Student B, completing the noun phrases with the options in the box below.

> It's hard to imagine the ¹_____ Rebel Wilson in any other career. Full of an energy ²_____ , she puts a smile on the face of anyone who watches her. Nobody who's seen the actress ³_____ in the *Pitch Perfect* movies can fail to be inspired by ⁴_____ presence.
>
> So it may come as a surprise to learn that she originally embarked on ⁵_____ path, and it was becoming seriously ill that changed her life forever!

> singing, dancing, and generally causing chaos
> a totally different
> popular Australian actor
> that brightens up the screen
> her joyful on-screen

2 Listen to Student B read the second part of the article. Check that he/she has correctly completed the noun phrases in **bold**.

> A highly intelligent woman, Rebel originally went to **college in Australia, where she studied law**. Everyone anticipated that she would have **a successful career working in a law firm**. However, she was on a trip to Mozambique when she became so sick with **the extremely unpleasant tropical disease of malaria** that she almost died. The drugs she was given caused strange dreams, including one in which she won an Oscar.
>
> Despite **her mother's great disappointment**, this vision clarified things in Rebel's mind. Now she knew for sure that she wanted to move to the U.S. and become an actor. But she did manage to justify **the law studies she never completed** – she was able to negotiate her own contracts!

5D Student A

1 Read sentences 1–5 to Student B. Listen to Student B's reaction. Why is he/she using repetition in each example?

1 I woke up at 4:30 this morning.
2 What do you think of Caesar's?
3 The capital of Brazil is Rio de Janeiro.
4 It's my birthday next week.
5 Which achievement are you most proud of?

2 Listen to Student B and respond with sentences a–e. Fill in the blanks by repeating some of his/her sentence. The reasons for repetition are in parentheses.

a The new _____ ? No, I haven't. But I've heard it's pretty good.
(to clarify)
b _____ ? Does he enjoy it?
(to show interest)
c _____ ? Sorry, but I'm busy then.
(to give yourself time to think)
d _____ ? You're joking!
(to show surprise)
e _____ ? It's 80 kilometers an hour.
(to correct)

COMMUNICATION PRACTICE

1A Student B

1 Look at the picture and read the story behind it.

- According to the most recent World Happiness report, the world's happiest country is Norway.
- Researchers have been collecting data on happiness since 2012 and publishing it in this annual report.
- The report is hoping to influence public policy and social progress around the world.
- In order to measure happiness, factors that are analyzed include life expectancy, social support, freedom of choice in decisions, and generosity.
- Other countries that have been included in the top twenty over the years are Canada, New Zealand, Costa Rica, Germany, Chile, and Brazil.

2 Look at Student A's picture and listen to the story behind it.

3 Cover the text and tell Student A the story behind your picture.

1C Student B

1 Listen to Student A's sentences and respond using the prompts.

1 A ...
   B No, it was Fred ...
2 A ...
   B Really? What I'm really ...
3 A ...
   B No, it was ... (wrong floor)
4 A ...
   B No, what I ...

2 Read your sentences and listen to Student A's responses.

1 B Sarah met Frank for a meal.
   A ...
2 B I'd like to go to Hawaii for a vacation.
   A ...
3 B She heard a strange noise coming from the basement.
   A ...
4 B My mother taught me a lot about understanding people.
   A ...

COMMUNICATION PRACTICE

1D Student B

1. Choose one of the topics below for Student A to talk about for one minute. How many types of fillers does he/she use?

   - the type of food you like
   - your friends in high school or college

2. Student A will give you a topic to talk about.

3. Talk about the topic for one minute without stopping. Use paraphrasing to emphasize and clarify, and fillers to avoid long pauses.

2A Student B

1. Read Simon's description of hot yoga classes.

Hot Yoga

I've been doing hot yoga for over two years now, and I love it! It's like normal yoga, except you do it in a hot, humid room. You sweat a lot, which is supposed to get rid of toxins in your kidneys, liver, and other internal organs. The heat also means you're less likely to pull a muscle. It's important not to eat for at least a couple of hours beforehand. Otherwise, you could feel nauseous. Also, you can't drink anything during the session, so it's important to have plenty of water afterward. If you have the time to do it twice a week, you'll quickly see the benefits.

2. Listen to Student A talking about veganism. Would you like to try this?

3. Cover the text. Tell Student B about hot yoga, using the prompts below.
   - Hot yoga should help to …
   - If you eat before hot yoga, you may …
   - After the lesson, you ought to …
   - You will get the most out of it if you can manage to …

COMMUNICATION PRACTICE

2C Student B

1. Student A will tell you three things about something that happened with his/her friend Matt. Respond after each point. Use the prompts a–c.

   a I'm not surprised you're angry. He should have … , but maybe you shouldn't have …
   b Perhaps it wasn't all his fault. He might have been … He could have … However, it's not a very nice thing to do. Maybe you should have …
   c I totally understand. You must be …

2. Use the information in the box to tell Student A about Pilar, a friend who is acting strangely. Add some details to your story to make it more realistic. Student A will respond after each point.

   1 Your friend Pilar has been acting rather strangely. You think something bad might have happened because she seems to be annoyed about something. You're concerned you may have done something to upset her.
   2 Every time you call her to make plans to get together, she makes an excuse, sounds very distant, and never asks you how you're doing any longer. Last time you called, she wouldn't speak to you at all.
   3 You texted her and told her she was being rude, and you demanded to know what was going on.

3A Student B

1. Look at the picture and read the story behind it.

LOST AND FOUND

Mary Grams, a Canadian farmer, was heartbroken when she lost the engagement ring she had been wearing for over 50 years. She was working in a field when she noticed that it had disappeared. She spent a long time searching for it, but without success. She was worried that her husband would be annoyed that she had lost it, so she bought a cheap replacement and used to wear that, instead. Luckily for her, he never noticed!

More than a decade later, her granddaughter came in with a very strange object that Mary's daughter-in-law had just dug up – a carrot with a ring around it! Mary recognized her engagement ring right away! She was delighted to have it back again, and even happier when her daughter-in-law admitted that she hadn't noticed the ring at first, and had almost fed the strangely shaped carrot to her dog!

2. Look at Student A's picture and listen to the story behind it.

3. Cover the text and tell Student A the story behind your picture.

COMMUNICATION PRACTICE

3C Student B

1 Read the takeout dessert menu.

Takeout Menu
Desserts

Fruit Fancy $7.99
Two scoops of sugar-free and low-fat frozen yogurt topped with a spectacular arrangement of fresh tropical fruits, this is what you've always wanted – a delicious dessert that is actually good for you! (350 calories)

Choctastic $10.99
Chunks of white chocolate cake and dark chocolate brownie topped with chocolate ice cream and swirls of milk chocolate, all topped with chocolate chips. To share with a friend or eat on your own if you dare! (930 calories)

Banana Boat $5.99
Deliciously simple vanilla ice cream served on two pan-fried bananas. Drizzled with salted caramel sauce and topped with chopped nuts. (700 calories)

2 Listen to Student A tell you about three pizzas on his/her takeout menu. Ask questions about the pizzas with the words and phrases in the box. Decide which pizza you want.

> biggest   thickest topping   least expensive
> least fattening   spiciest   tastiest

3 Tell Student A about the three desserts. Then answer Student A's questions. Use some of the expressions in the box.

> nowhere near as   by far the   far more   significantly less
> twice as   a good deal   not quite as   one of the

4A Student B

1 Listen to Student A telling you about the problem his/her friend Andy is having.

2 Choose six of the phrases in the box to give Student A some advice: three for things he/she should do and three for things he/she shouldn't do to help Andy.

> advise him   let him   make him   enough talent
> criticize him for   It's no good
> It might be a good idea   tell him

3 Tell Student B about the problem your friend Lucy is having. Use the information in the box.

Lucy wants to open her own restaurant, but she has very little money of her own, and nobody will give her a loan. She's convinced she'll make it, but she's never even worked in a restaurant, and the only cooking she does is for her roommates. Her goals are completely unrealistic, but she refuses to consider a different job. She's not very good at managing her own money. In fact, she can't even pay her rent this month.

4 Listen to Student A's advice. Respond by saying whether or not you think it is good advice or by asking for further explanation, if necessary.

COMMUNICATION PRACTICE

4C Student B

1 Listen to Student A's statements. Discuss whether you think they are true.

2 Read the statements. Discuss whether you think they are true.

> - Rarely do truly good people become world leaders.
> - Not only do Internet services cost an arm and a leg, they also run really slowly.
> - Not until you are at least twenty-five should you have children.
> - Only by traveling can you hope to understand other cultures.

5A Student B

1 Listen to Student A's questions. Choose the correct response a–e.

a We could, but I don't think he'll want to. He's been feeling a little down recently. Maybe we should visit him and then see what he wants to do.

b My friend Amy told me the Chinese place is fabulous, so let's try that one. If it's not, we can blame her!

c Oh, you shouldn't have! Thank you so much – I absolutely adore it!

d What? I didn't get an invitation to the wedding, did you? I suppose I wouldn't really expect to get one, but I would have thought you would.

e I'd love to, but I can't really afford it right now. I'll still come with you and help you choose one, though.

2 Ask Student A questions 1–5. Listen to his/her answers.

1 Do you have a car, and if so, how would you feel about driving me to the airport next Monday?

2 I need to borrow a lawnmower, but I don't know anyone who has one. Do you know anyone who does?

3 I'm thinking of making curry when Tara and Jamie come over for dinner. Do you know if they like spicy food? If not, I'll have to think of something else.

4 Do you know where I can buy good avocados? I need some nice ripe ones.

5 Our client wants this work done by Monday. I'm hoping to finish it on Friday, but if I don't, could you come in on Saturday to help me?

5C Student B

1 Listen to Student A read the first part of the article. Check that he/she has correctly completed the noun phrases in **bold**.

> It's hard to imagine **the popular Australian actor Rebel Wilson** in any other career. Full of **an energy that brightens up the screen**, she puts a smile on the face of anyone who watches her. Nobody who's seen **the actress singing, dancing, and generally causing chaos** in the *Pitch Perfect* movies can fail to be inspired by **her joyful on-screen presence**.
>
> So it may come as a surprise to learn that she originally embarked on **a totally different path**, and it was becoming seriously ill that changed her life forever!

2 Read the second part of the article to Student A, completing the noun phrases with the options in the box below.

> A highly intelligent woman, Rebel originally went to college [1]_____ . Everyone anticipated that she would have [2]_____ firm. However, she was on a trip to Mozambique when she became so sick with [3]_____ malaria that she almost died. The drugs she was given caused strange dreams, including one in which she won an Oscar.
>
> Despite [4]_____ disappointment, this vision clarified things in Rebel's mind. Now she knew for sure that she wanted to move to the U.S. and become an actor. But she did manage to justify the law [5]_____ – she was able to negotiate her own contracts!

> her mother's great
> a successful career working in a law
> studies she never completed
> the extremely unpleasant tropical disease of
> in Australia, where she studied law

145

COMMUNICATION PRACTICE

5D Student B

1 Listen to Student A and respond with sentences a–e. Fill in the blanks by repeating some of his/her sentence. The reasons for repetition are in parentheses.

a _____ ? Why?
(to show surprise)

b _____ as in the restaurant? It's OK, but there are nicer ones.
(to clarify)

c _____ ? No, it's Brasilia.
(to correct)

d _____ ? Are you doing anything nice?
(to show interest)

e _____ ? Probably passing my driving test.
(to give yourself time to think)

2 Read sentences 1–5 to Student A. Listen to Student A's reaction. Why is he/she using repetition in each example?

1 I'm going to watch the *X-Men* movie tonight. Have you seen it?
2 Did I ever tell you my cousin is a police officer?
3 Would you like to get together for coffee on Wednesday morning?
4 Did you know Patrick has six brothers?
5 The speed limit is 100 kilometers an hour here, isn't it?

American English

Personal Best

Workbook

C1 Advanced

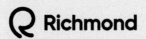

UNIT 1

What matters

1A LANGUAGE

GRAMMAR: The present: simple, continuous, and perfect aspects

1 Complete the sentences with the words in the box.

waters   is watering   's watered
's been watering   collect   'm collecting
've collected   've been collecting

1 Her shoes are muddy because she _____ the plants in her backyard.
2 I _____ stamps since I was a child.
3 My parents _____ antique china.
4 Mom's outside at the moment. I think she _____ her roses.
5 My neighbor always _____ my plants when I go on vacation.
6 Dan's getting married next month. I _____ money for a present for him.
7 We're asking people to donate money for the earthquake victims. We _____ over $300 already.
8 Ned _____ the vegetables in the backyard a couple of times in the past.

2 Complete the conversation with the correct form of the verbs in parentheses.

Marta Hi, Julia. Who was that on the phone?
Julia It was Matt. I ¹_____ (try) to persuade him to come on vacation with us.
Marta Has he agreed yet?
Julia No. The problem is that he's in a band, and they ²_____ (play) a lot of concerts at the moment. You know how much he ³_____ (love) his music.
Marta Yes, but I really ⁴_____ (think) he needs a rest. They ⁵_____ (do) at least fifteen shows in the last month, and he looks totally exhausted.
Julia Yes, and he ⁶_____ (study) for his exam in accounting since January, as well.
Marta Yes, that's true. Also, things ⁷_____ (be) very busy at his job recently.
Julia Yes, I know. It's all too much, isn't it? I must admit that I ⁸_____ (get) a bit worried about him.

VOCABULARY: Attitudes and emotions

3 Complete the phrases with the words in the box.

bright   into   ball   envy   moon   kept
threw   carried   come   earth

1 I was over the _____ when I learned I'd gotten the job.
2 I think Mom got a bit _____ away with the party decorations. There are balloons everywhere!
3 He was green with _____ when he saw my new phone.
4 The interview was very stressful, but he _____ his cool and made a very good impression.
5 I didn't get _____ horseback riding until I was 35.
6 I know you're sad about finishing college, but look on the _____ side. You won't have to worry about exams again.
7 Even though Jamie didn't know anyone at the party, he _____ himself into the celebrations enthusiastically.
8 She may be an international star, but she's still very down to _____ and does all her own shopping and housework.
9 He can _____ across as rude, but he's really just shy.
10 You need to be on the _____ in this business. Things can change very quickly.

4 Choose the correct options to complete the sentences.

1 We were *astonished / conscientious / disgusted* to discover that the building was over 500 years old.
2 When I saw how filthy the car was, I was absolutely *sarcastic / open-minded / disgusted*.
3 My parents have very traditional attitudes to family life. I wish they could be a bit more *courageous / thankful / open-minded*.
4 It was chilly in the evening, and I was *thankful / astonished / disgusted* for my jacket.
5 She said the food was really great, but I think she was being *conscientious / sarcastic / disgusted*.
6 He made the *thankful / courageous / sarcastic* decision to testify at the trial of his former friend.
7 Their *open-minded / conscientious / thankful* work led them to discover the company's illegal dealings.

PRONUNCIATION: /s/ and /z/

5 ▶1.1 Read the sentences. Is the *s* in **bold** pronounced with a /s/ or a /z/ sound? Circle the correct sound, and then listen and check.

1 Kate**'s** mountain bike cost $700!   /s/ /z/
2 It**'s** difficult to see the stage from here.   /s/ /z/
3 He**'s** asked me to have dinner with him.   /s/ /z/
4 Aunt Jane**'s** been showing me her vacation photos.   /s/ /z/
5 Philip**'s** washed all the dishes.   /s/ /z/

SKILLS 1B

READING: Dealing with non-literal language

Life lessons: Alice Greendale

Alice Greendale is one of the most in-demand actresses working at the moment. Known for her sharp intelligence, on-screen presence, and her ability to <u>get inside the skin</u> of the characters she plays, it is hard to believe that she was once a shy teenager whose self-esteem was so low that her drama teacher had to practically force her to take part in school plays.

What would you tell your 16-year-old self?
Believe in yourself! In those days, I was <u>eaten up</u> with self-doubt. I used to feel sick every week before drama class because I was desperate to do well, and yet my confidence was non-existent. I always knew I wanted to act, but it felt like a ridiculous dream for someone like me. If I'd known that one day I'd be standing on the Hollywood red carpet, it would have made such a difference!

What's the worst thing anyone's ever said to you?
"You're not beautiful enough to play Juliet." At the time, that was a real <u>slap in the face</u>, but I can laugh about it now. Failing to meet the beauty standards of a classic heroine has actually <u>opened many doors for me</u>. I've been so lucky with the range and variety of parts I've been offered.

When were you happiest?
On the set of *Time Zone*. For starters, we were filming in Kenya, which is such a spectacular country. But, more important, there was one photographer who was particularly <u>easy on the eyes</u>. Every evening, we'd sit together to watch those intense sunsets, and it was inevitable that we would fall in love. We <u>tied the knot</u> the following year and will celebrate our fifth wedding anniversary in June!

What's the most important lesson life has taught you?
To be myself. When I was younger, I was always <u>putting on an act</u>, and not just when I was working! For instance, I would dress for other people, rather than wear what I was comfortable in, or pretend to hold views that weren't mine, just to avoid causing offense. But it was only when I gained the confidence to show people the genuine me that my career really <u>got off the ground</u>.

1 Check (✓) the sentences that are true.

1 Alice Greendale was reluctant to take part in her school plays. _____
2 She was always sure that she would become a successful actor. _____
3 She still finds it hurtful that someone said she wasn't very beautiful. _____
4 She has always played the same type of role. _____
5 The happiest time of her life was while she was making a movie. _____
6 She didn't expect to fall in love while she was filming *Time Zone*. _____
7 When she was younger, other people used to tell her what to wear. _____
8 At that time, she was careful not to upset people with her opinions. _____

2 Look at the underlined phrases in the text. Choose the best ending for the definitions.

1 If you "get inside someone's skin," you
  a do a lot of research on the person.
  b understand the person's personality very well.
  c look a lot like the person.
2 If a feeling "eats you up," it
  a makes you feel very upset.
  b makes you physically unable to do anything.
  c makes you lose a lot of weight.
3 Something that is a "slap in the face," makes you feel
  a extremely angry.
  b shocked and upset.
  c very nervous.
4 If something "opens doors for you," it
  a makes your life easier.
  b forces you to change your plans.
  c gives you opportunities.
5 If a person is "easy on the eyes," he/she
  a is easy to see in a crowd of people.
  b is good at noticing things.
  c is physically attractive.
6 If you "tie the knot," you
  a get married.
  b start to live with someone.
  c get to know someone very well.
7 If you "put on an act," you
  a try to entertain people around you.
  b tell many lies.
  c behave in a false way.
8 If something "gets off the ground," it
  a becomes easier to do.
  b starts to be successful.
  c starts to become more enjoyable.

3 Choose the correct option to complete the sentences.

1 When I was little, my dad *was always reading / would read* me a bedtime story.
2 My sister *used to / would* live in Colorado.
3 We *attended / were always attending* a local school.
4 In those days, we *used to / would* know everyone in town.
5 We *would move / were always moving* because my parents were in the army.
6 My grandparents *would have / had* a house near a lake.

1C LANGUAGE

GRAMMAR: adding emphasis (1): cleft sentences

1 Choose the correct options to complete the sentences.

1 _____ I object to most is the cost of the tickets.
   a The person   b The main thing
   c What

2 _____ the younger students who cause the most trouble.
   a It's   b They're
   c The main thing is

3 _____ we argue about is whose turn it is to do the housework.
   a It's what   b The reason why
   c The main thing

4 _____ he wants is to have a chance to apologize.
   a The reason that   b All that
   c It's what

5 _____ influenced me most was my grandmother.
   a What   b The person who
   c The only thing that

6 _____ Lena who told me about the hidden room.
   a It was   b What
   c It's

7 _____ I chose this college was because of its sports facilities.
   a It was why   b The place
   c The reason

8 _____ really surprised me was how charming she was.
   a What   b The only thing
   c It was

2 Are these sentences correct or incorrect? Cross out any mistakes and write the correct words at the end of the sentences.

1 The only thing what he ever gave me was this ring. _____

2 It's my colleagues who make this such a great place to work. _____

3 The main that worries me is whether we'll have enough water. _____

4 What she really likes are the Italian paintings in the other gallery. _____

5 The place I love most is a small lake near my uncle's house. _____

6 The reason why he's upset is that his wife is sick. _____

7 They're our children who are the future. _____

8 It's I find fascinating is the way the artist paints the sky. _____

VOCABULARY: Abstract nouns

3 Complete the text with the abstract nouns in the box. There are two that you don't need.

> selfishness   hatred   tolerance   sensitivity   patience
> reliability   freedom   inconvenience   friendship   generosity

I met Laura when I started working at the restaurant where she was a chef. She was funny and kind, and we soon developed a close ¹_____. At the time, I was having trouble with my roommate, who kept leaving the place a mess even though she knew I liked it to be neat. I was increasingly fed up with her ²_____, and my ³_____ was running out. It got to the point where it was really getting me down. With her usual ⁴_____, Laura asked me what was wrong. When I told her, she immediately offered me her spare room. I was amazed by her ⁵_____, and I know it caused her considerable ⁶_____ because she had to move a lot of her stuff out of there to make room for me. It was supposed to be a temporary solution, but we get along so well that it's turning into a long-term one. We agree on pretty much everything – including our ⁷_____ of a messy place! In addition, the rent I pay gives her the ⁸_____ to travel, which she loves.

4 Complete the words.

1 The talk seemed to go on for hours, and none of it was relevant to me. I thought I would die of b_____!

2 There are three salespeople on our team, and we have a great working r_____.

3 She felt a great sense of p_____ when she heard how brave her son had been.

4 This job involves dealing with a lot of cash, so we need to be absolutely sure of the candidate's h_____.

5 The company I work for pays for my gym m_____.

6 Jake helped me a lot when I was sick, and I'm very grateful for his k_____.

7 She stood by me when everyone else was against me. Her l_____ was amazing.

8 Even as a child, she was always asking questions, and it was that c_____ that made her a great scientist.

9 My brother is so annoying. He shows absolutely no a_____ of other people's needs and feelings.

10 He hired a new manager, and his subsequent success has demonstrated the w_____ of that decision.

PRONUNCIATION: Intonation in cleft sentences

5 ▶1.2 Listen to the sentences. <u>Underline</u> the word that is stressed the most and pay attention to the falling intonation towards the end of the cleft clause.

1 It's their rudeness that makes me really angry.

2 It was the sauce that made it really delicious.

3 It was Brazil where we first met.

4 It wasn't Alex who took the money.

5 It was evening when he next contacted us.

6 It's traffic that causes most of the pollution here.

SKILLS 1D

SPEAKING: Paraphrasing

1 ▶ 1.3 Listen and check (✓) the phrases you hear.
1 Let me get this straight. _____
2 So what you mean is … Is that right? _____
3 In short … _____
4 So, the basic idea is … _____
5 Basically, … _____
6 What I think you're saying is … _____
7 In other words … _____
8 So, you're saying that … _____
9 Let me rephrase that … _____
10 Let me see, so … _____
11 Oh, I see, so … _____
12 So, what I mean is … _____

2 ▶ 1.3 Listen again and complete these sentences from the dialogue with the fillers the speakers use.
1 But you worked all last weekend, didn't you, and now, _____, you're planning to work all this weekend, as well?
2 _____, it might not be so easy when I'm older, especially if I have a family.
3 _____, yes, that's right.
4 If you keep ignoring us, we might just give up on you in the end, _____?
5 It's only been, _____, two or three weeks.
6 My manager is leaving in June, and I _____ think that if I can prove myself now, I'll have a good chance of getting her job.
7 I want to make sure that doesn't happen to my kids, _____.
8 I've never really _____. I can't imagine having a family for years.
9 Oh, _____! How about both?

3 Choose the correct options to complete the conversation.
A My dad's feeling down at the moment. [1]*Let's see, / Basically*, he's hurt his back, and it's really affecting his work. He's a sales rep, and he usually drives everywhere, so it's a real problem, [2]*you know what I mean / like*? And it makes him [3]*basically / kind of* walk strangely.
B That must be tough. My mom sometimes goes to an osteopath who's really good. He's on, [4]*um, / you see*, Carter Street, I think, and his name's Martin Young.
A What does an osteopath actually do? I've never been to one, [5]*like / you know*.
B [6]*Oh, that's a hard one, / Basically*, but from what Mom tells me, I think they try to, [7]*you know what I mean, / basically*, move your bones and muscles and stuff into the right position.
A [8]*Hmm, / Let's see*, I'm not sure my dad could afford it, to be honest. Is it, [9]*you see, / like*, really expensive?
B [10]*That's a good question. / Oh, that's a hard one*. I'll find out and let you know.

4 Use your own ideas to complete the conversation.
A If I have to do something difficult at work, for example, let's see, giving a presentation or something like that, I find it really helps to wear something attractive. Or, to put it another way, _____.
B So, what you're saying is that if you look confident, you feel confident.
A Exactly. Don't you find that?
B I've never really thought about it before. _____.
A I think clothes are really important. They tell you so much about a person.
B So, what you mean is _____. Is that right?
A Yes, in my opinion, if people don't make an effort with their clothes, they won't make an effort with other things. That is to say, _____.
B Let me see, so _____. But what if you can't afford the perfect clothes for each different occasion?
A That's a good question. But even chain-store clothes are pretty good these days. In other words, _____.
B I get it, I'd better put on my best clothes the next time I come to your house!

5

1 REVIEW and PRACTICE

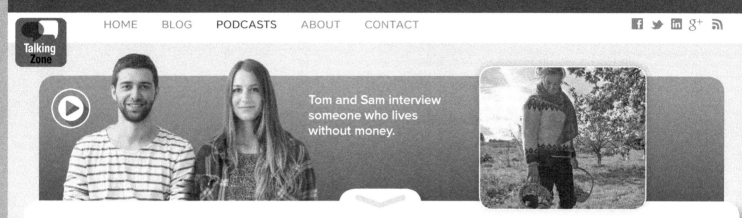

HOME BLOG **PODCASTS** ABOUT CONTACT

Tom and Sam interview someone who lives without money.

LISTENING

1 ▶ 1.4 Listen to the podcast and choose the best summary.

a Sophie lives with a woman who gives her most of what she needs. She is worried about picking food because it may be poisonous or polluted. She doesn't think she will continue without money forever.

b Sophie doesn't use money at the moment, although she may in the future. She has found ways to get food and housing without spending money.

c Sophie doesn't use money, but she says that her lifestyle is not always easy. It is difficult for her to get enough to eat, and she would not expect her future children to live without money.

2 ▶ 1.4 Listen again. Are the sentences true (T), false (F) or doesn't say (DS)?

1 Sophie works for other people in return for cash. _____
2 She likes the place where she lives. _____
3 She doesn't eat meat. _____
4 According to Sophie, most wild food is poisonous. _____
5 It's dangerous to pick food by a busy highway. _____
6 Sophie's lifestyle helps her stay in shape. _____
7 She wishes she could give her family expensive birthday presents. _____
8 She wants her children to understand how money can affect the environment. _____

READING

1 Read Sam's blog on page 7 quickly. Match paragraphs A–F with summaries 1–6.

1 Sam was amazed that Charlotte felt so jealous of her sister. _____
2 Sam was sad because she had upset her friend. _____
3 Sam wants to continue to be friends with Charlotte. _____
4 Charlotte received a vase as a gift. _____
5 Fairness is also important to monkeys. _____
6 Different people define fairness in different ways. _____

2 Choose the correct options to complete the sentences.

1 Sam reacted to what Charlotte told her by saying things that showed she
 a didn't understand what Charlotte had said.
 b thought that Charlotte was joking.
 c didn't think Charlotte's anger was reasonable.
2 Charlotte's aunt was giving things away because
 a she won't have as much space in her new home.
 b she wanted to make her nieces happy.
 c they're not suitable for a modern apartment.
3 Charlotte has always loved the vase her aunt gave her, but
 a she really wanted to have the piano.
 b she was annoyed because her sister received a more valuable gift.
 c she thinks she should have been given something better than her sister.
4 Sam thinks Charlotte's feelings are unreasonable because
 a her sister will be able to use the piano, and she won't.
 b she loves her sister and should be pleased for her.
 c she has always wanted the vase.
5 When she looked on the Internet, Sam realized that this type of jealous behavior is due to
 a events that happened during our childhood.
 b the way our brains have developed.
 c the fact that we are physically incapable of controlling our emotions.
6 The fact that people have different ideas about fairness means that
 a governments need to make sure that everyone is treated equally.
 b governments need to prevent them from fighting about it.
 c it is difficult for them to agree about political decisions.

6

REVIEW and PRACTICE 1

HOME BLOG PODCASTS ABOUT CONTACT

Sam writes about the idea of fairness.

That's so unfair!

We all seem to have an built-in sense of what is fair and what's not fair in life, but do we all have the same idea of what fairness is? Apparently not! A recent disagreement has reminded me that even close friends have different ideas of fairness.

A I was feeling a bit down earlier. The reason I felt bad was that I upset my close friend Charlotte last night by making some sarcastic comments about something she told me. Something that seemed so childish to me I could hardly believe I was hearing it, but which she obviously felt so outraged about that my lack of sensitivity genuinely hurt her.

B So, Charlotte's aunt is moving from her enormous farmhouse to a small apartment, and she's been going through all the stuff she needs to get rid of. She came over to Charlotte's to give her an antique vase that Charlotte's always loved. You'd think that Charlotte would be pleased by her aunt's generosity. But no, instead of being thankful, she's green with envy because her aunt is giving her sister her grand piano, and that's worth far more than the vase.

C I was astonished at her reaction, and I'm afraid I let it show. Charlotte has gained something lovely that she didn't have before. Why can't she just be happy for her sister? After all, the piano has to go somewhere. What shocked me most was that Charlotte doesn't even play the piano! It's fair to say that our evening ended awkwardly, and we didn't share our usual hug when we said good-bye.

D My friendship with Charlotte is important to me, and after a good night's sleep, I wondered if I'd been a little hard on her. When I googled "fairness," I discovered that it is, indeed, incredibly important to us, and it may be more of a biological thing than we realize. It seems that even monkeys display similar behavior to Charlotte. In one study, a monkey was taught to give the researcher a rock, and received a cucumber in return. At first, the monkey was content with that, but it was when it saw a neighboring monkey being rewarded with a (much more desirable) grape that the trouble began. From then on, when the first monkey was given a cucumber, it would throw it back at the researcher and shake the cage in fury.

E So even monkeys care about fairness. However, there is little agreement about what fairness consists of. Apparently, there are three main ideas, which can be summed up as "sameness," "deservedness," or "need." In other words, some people think that everyone should be equal, some that we should be rewarded according to effort, and some that we should help those who need it most. When you think about how basic, yet conflicting, those concepts are, and the implications they have for governments, it's no wonder we argue about politics!

F Anyway, I feel better now that I know that what I saw as Charlotte's selfishness may not be entirely under her control. I hope we'll be able to mend our relationship, but I guess that telling her she's acting like a monkey may not be the best way to go about it!

7

UNIT 2 Live better

2A LANGUAGE

GRAMMAR: Modal verbs (1) and modal-like forms

1 Complete each sentence with a word from the box.

> had   should   managed   need
> prepared   can't   better   supposed

1 She's not _____ to eat sugar on her new diet.
2 You'll _____ to hurry if you want to see her.
3 I might not be back in time for the doctor's appointment. I'd _____ reschedule it.
4 Sophie let me borrow her phone, so I really _____ lose it!
5 You _____ speak to Joe about visiting Vietnam. He's been there twice.
6 Eventually, he _____ to pass his driving test.
7 I'm not _____ to pay $700 for a new jacket!
8 She _____ better not be late this time!

2 Complete the second sentence so that it means the same as the first sentence. Use the correct form of the words and phrases in the box.

> be likely to   be (not) supposed to   had better (not)
> be (not) prepared to   (don't) need to   manage to

1 Josh is unreliable, so I'm not willing to trust him.
Josh is unreliable, so I'm _____
_____

2 Fortunately, we succeeded in getting home before the storm started.
Fortunately, we _____
_____

3 My doctor says that I shouldn't eat high-fat foods like cheese and butter.
My doctor says that I _____
_____

4 Your mom will be worried, so you should call her and tell her you're safe.
Your mom will be worried, so you _____
_____

5 By the time he arrives, he'll probably be very hungry.
By the time he arrives, he _____
_____

6 You can come tonight, but it's not necessary if you don't want to.
You can come tonight but you _____
_____

VOCABULARY: Health and medical treatment

3 Choose the correct options to complete the sentences.

1 If you cut yourself badly, you may have to have *stitches / side effects*.
2 The curved bones that go from your chest to your back are called your *spine / ribs*.
3 You use your *kidneys / lungs* to breathe.
4 I have a *blister / bruise* on my heel from my boots.
5 I *pulled / picked up* a muscle in my leg while I was playing tennis, and it's so painful.
6 You should put a *Band-Aid / cast* on that cut.
7 I put a *blister / bandage* around my knee to support it.
8 She fell and *pulled / sprained* her ankle.

4 Complete the sentences with the correct words.

1 A very bad headache is a s_____ headache.
2 If you are a_____ to something, you become sick when you eat, touch, or breathe it.
3 A medical problem that is caused by taking medication is called a s_____ e_____ .
4 To see whether you have broken a bone, you may have to have an X-_____.
5 An illness affecting your stomach is sometimes called an u_____ stomach.
6 If you get an infection, take a_____ .
7 His doctor arranged for a brain s_____ to check that there was no damage.
8 I felt so d_____ when I stood up that I thought I was going to faint.
9 I p_____ u_____ a bug while I was on vacation and came home sick.
10 My dad has high blood p_____ .

PRONUNCIATION: linking modal-like forms with *to*

5 ▶ 2.1   Read the sentences aloud. Notice the way that the consonant sounds /t/ and /d/ combine with the /t/ in the word *to*. Listen and repeat.

1 You're not suppose**d t**o walk on the grass.
2 Are you prepare**d t**o pay for the treatment?
3 You don't nee**d t**o fill out all the forms.
4 You ough**t t**o speak to Dan about the problem.
5 He manage**d t**o climb out of the window.

SKILLS 2B

LISTENING: Understanding attitude and opinion

1 ▶ 2.2 Listen to a conversation between Anna and Enrico and choose the best options.

1 Most days, Anna goes for walk
 a in the country.
 b in the park.
 c around her neighborhood.

2 Enrico claims that a lot of people
 a do not see nature in their daily lives.
 b are not interested in nature.
 c prefer technology to nature.

3 Anna makes the point that
 a cities are full of nature.
 b there is no nature in cities.
 c there is some nature in cities.

4 Enrico says that we should
 a notice the nature around us, even in the city.
 b go to places where there is a lot of nature.
 c put more trees and green spaces in cities.

5 Anna says she sometimes
 a walks around the area where she lives.
 b goes for a walk in the country.
 c feels depressed.

6 Enrico says that according to research, walking
 a in the country decreases stress levels.
 b anywhere decreases stress levels.
 c has no effect on stress levels.

2 ▶ 2.2 Listen again. Complete the sentences.

1 And, um, _____? How is "green therapy" different from taking a walk in the park?

2 _____ some people benefit from those things.

3 _____ that people who live in cities spend most of their lives in buildings.

4 And, _____, even when they're outside, they're looking at the screens in their hands.

5 And the nature that you talk about in cities – _____, a lot of that is artificial.

6 Sure, but, _____, it's not the same as being out in nature and really spending time there.

7 _____ the country, but, occasionally, when I'm stressed …

3 ▶ 2.3 Listen to these sentences. Pay attention to the word with the underlined /ə/ sound. Notice how the sound disappears in fast speech. Listen and repeat.

1 He wasn't capable of rati<u>o</u>nal thought.
2 She studied hist<u>o</u>ry in college.
3 Her mother was a jew<u>e</u>ler.
4 Both children are making satisfact<u>o</u>ry progress.
5 They played the nati<u>o</u>nal anthem.
6 What's the diff<u>e</u>rence in meaning?

4 Complete the words in these sentences using the anagrams in parentheses to help you.

1 From time to time, we all experience disappointment, and we have to learn how to _____ it. (nadhle)

2 I thought she showed a bit of _____ in trying to find a solution to the problem herself. (niitaiivet)

3 Unfortunately, residents of the area refused to _____ with the police. (reapoocet)

4 When we're suffering from stress, we're sometimes less able to _____ with everyday problems. (adle)

5 Sometimes a project is so hard that you want to give up, but you have to _____. (srepeerev)

6 I had three small children and a very demanding job and was finding it difficult to _____. (opec)

7 He took a course at work to learn how to _____ his time. (namega)

8 I've set myself a _____. I'm going to lose six kilos by December. (lago)

9 A team of writers will _____ on the script for the movie. (loclabroate)

10 Sometimes she finds it hard to _____ her workload. (riporiitez)

11 Holly decided to _____ the initiative and set up a club herself. (keat)

9

2C LANGUAGE

GRAMMAR: Modal verbs (2): advanced forms

1 Choose the correct options to complete the sentences.

1 You can't _____ hungry already! You just ate!
   a have felt   **b** be feeling   **c** to be feeling

2 I borrowed some chairs for the party, but no one sat, so I _____.
   a needn't have bothered
   b needn't bothered   **c** needn't bother

3 Excellent news! William got 95% on the test. He _____ been disappointed!
   a can't have   **b** can't   **c** must have

4 No one's here. Everyone must _____ already.
   a leave   **b** have been leaving   **c** have left

5 James should _____ his room, but, instead, he was sunbathing in the backyard!
   a be cleaning   **b** have been cleaning
   c clean

6 They may not want food when they arrive. They might _____ already.
   a have been eating   **b** be eating
   c have eaten

7 Why were you talking when the teacher was speaking? You should _____ listening!
   a to be   **b** have been   **c** to have been

8 Isabel doesn't have much money. She shouldn't _____ for us!
   a to be paying   **b** be paying
   c have paying

2 Complete the second sentence so that it means the same as the first sentence.

1 Perhaps Anna was visiting her sister.
   Anna might _____.

2 I'm sure he's not walking the whole way! It's 30 miles!
   He can't _____.

3 It's possible that Rosie has already told him the news.
   Rosie may already _____.

4 It was a bad idea of yours to invite so many people.
   You shouldn't _____.

5 Maybe he was hiding from Alex.
   He could _____.

6 Rebecca brought extra blankets, but there was no need for them.
   Rebecca needn't _____.

7 Surely she wasn't talking about Tom!
   She can't _____.

8 I regret that I upset her.
   I shouldn't _____.

VOCABULARY: Verbs and nouns with the same form

3 Choose the correct options to complete the sentences.

1 When she decided to change jobs, she didn't do herself any *benefit* / *harm*.

2 Can you give us *a balance* / *an update* on the plans for the new highway?

3 The financial crisis had a big *impact* / *harm* on the country's economy.

4 I *regretted* / *envied* my cousin because he was better off and more successful than me.

5 At the moment, Adam's *focusing* / *sacrificing* on his exams.

6 The boy's poor grades in school gave his parents cause for *regret* / *concern*.

7 It's very important to have a good work-life *balance* / *escape*.

8 When the passengers saw smoke coming from the wing, some of them started to *concern* / *panic*.

4 Complete each pair of sentences with the correct form of one of the words from exercise 3.

1 Stress had a negative _____ on my health.
   The war has _____ negatively on food production.

2 Her _____ is very much on her career.
   Jack really needs to _____ on his studies.

3 She gave us an _____ on the company's performance.
   Perhaps you could _____ us on your progress?

4 She made her _____ through a window.
   He managed to _____ from prison twice.

5 All parents make _____ for their children.
   My mother _____ her career for her family.

6 A _____ of being an only child is that your parents have a lot of time for you.
   He _____ financially when his father died.

7 One of my _____ is not having children.
   I certainly _____ being so rude to her.

8 I went into a terrible _____ when I lost my passport.
   I felt I couldn't breathe and started to _____.

PRONUNCIATION: Stress patterns with modal verb forms

5 ▶ 2.4 Listen to the sentences and underline the words with the most stress in the verb phrases in **bold**. Listen and repeat.

1 I **must be doing** this all wrong!

2 They **can't have left** already!

3 He **might not be benefiting** from the course.

4 I **needn't have worried** about not being smart enough!

5 He **should have told** Alice.

6 She **might have been sleeping** when I called.

10

SKILLS 2D

WRITING: Giving constructive criticism

1 Read the e-mail. Underline three sentences in which the author achieves a sense of balance by including a good point, as well as a negative one.

> To the organizers,
>
> I'd been looking for a course on plant-based cooking for some time, and so was excited to see "Plant-based health: a three-day cooking-for-health course" offered on your restaurant's website. I signed up immediately and attended the course in February. I've been a big fan of your vegan restaurant for years now, but I'm sorry to say that the course wasn't **quite** as described.
>
> The first morning ("Knife skills") went well enough. Louis, our very patient instructor, informed me that I'd been holding my knife wrong all these years and taught me the correct way to do it. However, Monday afternoon wasn't **quite** as productive. After an excellent plant-based lunch (the food each day was **quite** tasty), the session started with a discussion on the right and wrong way to do food production. Although Louis and your head chef, Ellie, were interesting and very well informed on the subject, I'm afraid this wasn't what I wanted from the course. Half an hour – or more – was spent discussing this issue, and I have to say that I wasn't the only participant who was impatient to get cooking! The moral issues around plant-based cooking are, of course, important to a lot of people, but perhaps they could form the basis of a different course?
>
> When we eventually started cooking on Monday afternoon, I was **quite** surprised to learn that we would be preparing desserts. Both dishes turned out well, and we all enjoyed eating them, but the recipes included large quantities of sugar and fat, substances that can't really be described as healthy. I'm sure there is a demand for plant-based cooking of this type, but I suggest that you cater to it with a different course – "plant-based treats" or something along those lines.
>
> Finally, at a cooking program that I attended in New York last year, the participants were each given a booklet of recipes at the end of the course. I've used this booklet many times, and it serves as a useful reminder of everything that I learned. Could I suggest that you also provide one in the future?
>
> Regards, Sarah Miller

2 Sarah was not happy with various aspects of the course. Check (✓) the aspects that she mentions.

1 The title and content of the course didn't match. ___
2 The instructor spent too long teaching them how to hold a knife. ___
3 Too little time was spent cooking. ___
4 She disagreed with the instructors' views on food production. ___
5 She felt that some of the dishes they cooked were not appropriate. ___

3 Find three polite suggestions in the text and write the phrases that introduce these suggestions.

1 _____
2 _____
3 _____

4 Match the examples of *quite* from the text (1–4) with uses a or b.

1 I'm sorry to say that the course wasn't quite as described. ___
2 Monday afternoon wasn't quite as productive. ___
3 The food each day was quite tasty. ___
4 I was quite surprised to learn that we would be preparing desserts. ___

a before an adjective of degree, meaning "fairly" or "pretty"
b in a phrase that "softens" a negative opinion

5 Use your own ideas to complete the sentences.

1 From the outside, the restaurant looked attractive and inviting. Sadly, _____

2 Despite the fact that the gym was spacious and well equipped, it _____

3 The teacher struggled to cope with so many students, and I feel _____

4 Although the instructors were friendly and charming, they _____

5 If you offer this course again, I'd suggest _____

6 Nobody, myself included, was wearing the appropriate clothing. Perhaps next time, _____

6 Imagine that a friend of yours owns a health food restaurant that you think could be improved. Write a polite and encouraging e-mail giving him/her some constructive criticism.

- Be encouraging by including positive points, as well as negative ones.
- Introduce your criticisms with "softening" phrases so that you don't sound rude.
- Avoid phrases that are extreme or very direct.
- Give at least one specific example of something that you think could be improved.
- Make at least one positive suggestion for improving the thing that you are criticizing.

11

2 REVIEW and PRACTICE

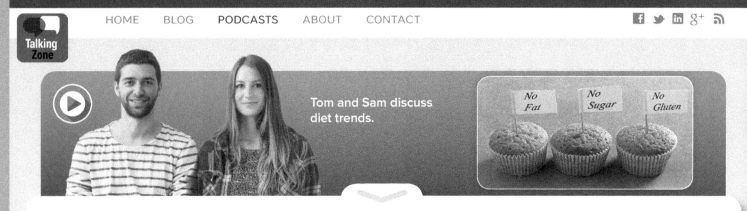

LISTENING

1 ▶ 2.5 Listen to the podcast. Check [✓] the best summary of Sam's discussion topic.

1 the benefits of not eating particular foods ____
2 the growing trend toward diets that do not include particular food items ____
3 the moral objections to eating particular foods ____

2 ▶ 2.5 Listen again. Do Sam and Tom say these things? Circle Y (Yes) or N (No).

1 Sam says that what she is talking about today cannot be accurately described as "fads." Y / N
2 She wants to focus on people who avoid certain foods because they are allergic to them. Y / N
3 Vegans and vegetarians tend to be young people. Y / N
4 Some people don't eat certain foods because they consider them to be unhealthy. Y / N
5 In the past, people didn't worry at all about how much sugar they ate. Y / N
6 The only reason some people don't eat bread is because they are allergic to wheat. Y / N
7 All of Sam's recent dinner guests were avoiding a particular food. Y / N
8 She didn't enjoy cooking for these people. Y / N
9 Sam agrees that the Internet has had an influence on people's diets. Y / N
10 Tom reminds Sam that wealth has also influenced diet. Y / N

READING

1 Read Sophia's blog on page 13 and number topics a–e in the order that they appear (1–5).

a a list of the possible advantages of meditation ____
b Sophia's problems that she hopes meditation might cure ____
c Sophia admitting that she finds it hard to give her attention to one thing ____
d another person's evidence that meditation can improve physical conditions ____
e Sophia's expectations for a previous meditation course ____

2 Are the sentences true (T), false (F), or doesn't say (DS)?

1 Sophia doubts that meditation has any real advantages. ____
2 She suspects that Joey's headaches were not cured by meditation. ____
3 Joey recommended a meditation course to her. ____
4 She finds it difficult to relax and often worries about things. ____
5 She suffers from stress. ____
6 At the moment, she finds it quite hard to concentrate on things. ____
7 She thinks the meditation course is expensive. ____
8 The people who attended the previous course seemed to find it useful. ____
9 The last meditation classes she attended helped her feel more relaxed. ____
10 When she attended the previous course, she was finding work especially stressful. ____

12

REVIEW and PRACTICE 2

HOME   BLOG   PODCASTS   ABOUT   CONTACT

Guest blogger Sophia writes about her attempts to silence her 'inner monkeys."

Inner peace and harmony?

I'll start with a confession, readers. I'm a meditation failure. Three times I've attended meditation classes in the attempt to calm my busy mind, and three times I've failed. Is it me, or have I just been going to the wrong classes?

Actually, one of my best friends (Joey) is living proof of the value of meditation. For six years, he'd suffered from splitting headaches, and no pill that the doctor ever prescribed could begin to cure them. Three months into a course on meditation last year, the headaches suddenly disappeared. Coincidence? Joey doesn't think so, and I'm inclined to believe him.

Once again, I find myself consulting the website of our local meditation center. Luckily, I don't suffer from headaches, but I am, I think it's accurate to say, a rather anxious person. Relaxation doesn't come easily to me. I also know that high blood pressure runs in my family – both of my parents suffer from it – so a therapy that might help me manage that particular medical condition probably makes sense. I'm looking at the various benefits here: "Meditation can reduce stress or, at least, help you handle the stress in your life." (This is certainly something that I could benefit from!) "It can increase happiness and positive emotions and boost your powers of concentration." (Yes, please!) The last of these would be especially beneficial. I find myself getting distracted very easily these days ...

So should I sign up for their eight-week course? What's the worst that could happen? I would sacrifice a fairly modest sum of money and would be giving up my Thursday evenings for no gain. That wouldn't be too much of a sacrifice, would it? Surely, it's worth a try. And yet ...

I find myself thinking back to my last failed attempt, and my enthusiasm instantly evaporates. I must have been doing it all wrong. The peace and calm of the meditation room that helped everyone around me achieve deep relaxation had exactly the opposite effect on me. While others cleared their minds of thoughts, I suddenly seemed to have a hundred worries: Where did I put my keys? Why didn't Isabel call? How was I going to meet that work deadline? (These thoughts are the chattering monkeys that make up the so-called "monkey mind.") And the more I tried to dismiss these chattering monkeys, the more loudly they insisted on being heard. I realize that I may have been hoping for too much from that class, but I was actually more stressed at the end of it than I had been at the start.

Readers, what do you think? Should I give it one last try?

13

Looking back

3A LANGUAGE

GRAMMAR: Past time

1 Are these sentences correct or incorrect? Cross out any mistakes and write the correct words at the end of the sentences.

1. I couldn't go to sleep because my neighbors had a noisy party. _____
2. We used to take lots of vacations because my parents retired by then. _____
3. I was terrified when we stayed in the castle because I would believe it had ghosts. _____
4. Did Izzie used to like dolls when she was younger? _____
5. By the time the police arrived, the thieves had been escaping. _____
6. Dan was always complaining because he had to work such long hours. _____
7. I had no idea that Sara looked for me. What did she want? _____
8. While Dad was talking to his friend, I wandered around the gardens. _____

2 Complete the text with the correct form of the verbs in parentheses. There may be more than one correct answer.

It was a hot summer day, and the sun ¹_____ (shine) brightly, so we ²_____ (decide) to ride our bikes to the nearest beach. In those days, we ³_____ (love) swimming in the ocean even though our parents ⁴_____ always _____ (warn) us to be careful of the high tides. My dad ⁵_____ (drag) out to sea by the tide once when he was a teenager and only ⁶_____ (survive) because two guys who ⁷_____ (fish) in a small boat nearby ⁸_____ (rescue) him. Before that day, I ⁹_____ never _____ (have) a problem with the ocean at that particular beach, but that day, the waves ¹⁰_____ (crash) violently against the shore. To our horror, our friend Max, who ¹¹_____ always _____ (do) stupid things, ¹²_____ (tear) off his clothes and ran right in.

VOCABULARY: Change and time

3 Complete the sentences with the correct form of the words in the box. There are four that you do not need.

> transition   millennium   obsolete   adapt to
> modify   die out   switch   transformation
> an era   stabilize   adjustment   decade

1. After rising by 25% over the last ten years, prices have _____ now.
2. Tom lived in Argentina for over two _____.
3. Our farm has recently _____ to organic methods.
4. I was amazed by the area's _____ into a vacation resort.
5. We help students make the _____ from high school to college.
6. He's struggled to _____ life in a totally different culture.
7. Future transactions will be made electronically, and cash will become _____.
8. We are living in _____ in which technology is developing quickly.

4 Complete the sentences with the missing words.

1. This chart shows the events in chronological _____.
2. I don't think astronauts will land on Mars in my _____.
3. Our house was built at the _____ of the twentieth century.
4. February is a day longer when it's a _____ year.
5. I know studying is hard, but it will be worth it in the long _____.
6. By then, silent movies had begun to go out of _____, and he found it difficult to get work.
7. In those _____, people often left their homes unlocked.
8. Since you can't find a hotel, you can stay with me for the time _____.

PRONUNCIATION: Weak forms of *had* and *been*

5 ▶ 3.1 Read the sentences aloud, paying particular attention to the pronunciation of *had* and *been* in the past perfect continuous. Listen and repeat.

1. I could tell that Mike and Sue had been arguing.
2. Marcos had been expecting a pay raise.
3. We wondered if David had been waiting for us.
4. We discovered that Matt had been lying to us.
5. I think his grandparents had been living abroad.
6. María had been carrying a heavy suitcase, so she was tired.

14

SKILLS 3B

READING: Understanding text structure and organization

An ordinary life?

1. One of my most treasured possessions is a photograph of my great-aunt, Nora Robinson, taken at her shoe factory. Nora's strong features have an expression of quiet pride – one that is richly deserved.

2. Born in 1935 to a miner and a shopkeeper, there was nothing in Nora's upbringing to indicate that she ¹_____ the conventional life of women of that era – marriage, children, and housework – in favor of a lifelong campaign for a cause she believed in.

3. The town where she grew up (with her sister Margaret, my grandmother) was struggling economically. Families were worn down by poverty. They desperately needed employment, but there wasn't any. Consequently, crime – especially theft – was high, and, of course, people caught stealing reduced their chances of getting a job even further.

4. Nora ²_____ how she became determined to break this negative cycle, following the imprisonment of an old childhood friend, by providing him with work. She knew he wasn't a bad person, but just a victim of circumstance, and she was aware that there must be many others in the same situation.

5. Clearly a very persuasive young woman, she began a campaign of visiting or writing pleading letters to all the wealthy families in the area and, as a result, managed to scrape together just enough money to open a small workshop making heavy leather boots. At first, she employed one experienced shoemaker and three ex-prisoners, who were left with no doubt that this was their one and only chance to turn their lives around. Gradually, the business grew, and Nora ³_____ around 50 people in the factory she was eventually able to build.

6. Nora was never famous, and she was never rich, so you might say that she had an ordinary life. However, she gave hope and opportunity to so many people who had had none, and her factory ⁴_____ a model for several similar initiatives elsewhere. Therefore, I'm very proud to claim that my great-aunt was a truly extraordinary person!

---

1 Read about Nora Robinson's life. Match phrases a–d with blanks 1–4.

a would later explain _____
b was to become _____
c would go on to employ _____
d was destined to reject _____

2 Are the sentences true (T), false (F), or doesn't say (DS)?

1 In her great niece's photo, Nora looks pleased with what she has achieved. _____
2 Nora's parents encouraged her to be different from other girls her age. _____
3 In the town where she grew up, crime was often linked to poverty. _____
4 It was a personal experience that made Nora want to help ex-prisoners. _____
5 Nora only hired people if she was certain they wouldn't commit another crime. _____
6 Rich people gave her the money to build her factory. _____
7 She got the idea for her factory from hearing about similar businesses elsewhere. _____
8 The people Nora helped were very grateful to her. _____

3 Find the organizing words or phrases in the text for doing the following:

1 Paragraph 2: introducing an alternative _____
2 Paragraph 3: showing a result _____
3 Paragraph 4: showing a method _____
4 Paragraph 5: showing a result _____
5 Paragraph 6: showing a result _____
6 Paragraph 6: showing a contrast _____
7 Paragraph 6: showing a result _____

4 Look at these sentences from the text. Underline the places where pronouns are used or words are omitted. Then write the full form at the end of the sentence.

1 Instead, her strong features have an expression of quiet pride – one that is richly deserved. _____

2 They desperately needed employment, but there wasn't any. _____

3 She knew he wasn't a bad person, but just a victim of circumstance, and she was aware that there must be many others in the same situation. _____

4 However, she gave hope and opportunity to so many people who had had none … _____

15

3C LANGUAGE

GRAMMAR: Comparison

1 Complete each sentence with one or two adjectives from the box. Add *as*, *than*, *the*, or *and* where they are needed.

> better effective expensive harder
> most dangerous steeper (x2) apologetic
> friendlier angrier

1 This restaurant is a good deal _____ _____ the one we ate in last night.
2 This medicine isn't quite _____ _____ _____ the stuff I took before.
3 Rick is a lot _____ _____ his brother.
4 _____ more _____ she was, _____ _____ the man seemed to get.
5 The mountain became _____ _____ _____ as we got near the top.
6 Things aren't nearly _____ _____ here _____ they are at home.
7 This is by far _____ _____ thing I've ever done in my life.
8 I think that German is much _____ _____ Spanish because of the grammar.

2 Use the prompts to complete the sentences.

1 Why don't you get a second-hand phone? It would be _____ .
   (considerably / cheap / a new one)
2 I really like Ms. Jones. She's _____ I've ever had.
   (by far / good / teacher)
3 She can swim a length in 40 seconds. That's _____ !
   (almost / twice / fast / me)
4 Max has lots of friends. He's _____ .
   (far / popular / Alex)
5 I hate swimming in the ocean and _____ to go in!
   (cold / it is / less likely / I am)
6 Julia says she finds riding a bike exhausting, but I find jogging _____ .
   (a lot / tiring / riding a bike)
7 My parents never used to yell at my sister, even though she was _____ .
   (just / naughty / me)
8 I really need to relax because _____ .
   (stressed / I am / bad / I sleep)

VOCABULARY: Expressions with *come* and *go*

3 Match sentences 1–8 with a–h.

1 Sara says her cat has disappeared. _____
2 He finds talking to strangers a real struggle. _____
3 Our vacation was kind of stressful, actually. _____
4 I suspected that Lucas had broken the window. _____
5 There's a problem with our website. _____
6 My uncle told me a bit about the show. _____
7 Ollie must be tired by now. _____
8 His wife says he's always at work. _____

   a He eventually came clean a couple of months later.
   b He didn't go into detail.
   c It went missing some time this morning.
   d It always seems to come first for him.
   e He's been on the go all day.
   f It doesn't come easily to him at all.
   g Nothing went according to plan.
   h It came to light yesterday.

4 Fill in the blanks in the conversation.

A Did you hear that Eva's business is in trouble?
B No! I thought, it was going from strength ¹_____ . What went ²_____ ?
A Apparently, she's come ³_____ a lot of problems importing the materials she needs.
B I can imagine. When it ⁴_____ to customs regulations, nothing's ever easy, is it?
A No, and their main supplier says he needs them to pay in advance, so they have more problems still to ⁵_____ . They only have enough materials to keep them ⁶_____ for two more months. She says that she's been going around in ⁷_____ trying to find a solution, but it seems hopeless.
B Oh, poor thing. Nothing ever goes ⁸_____ to plan, does it?
A No, it doesn't. Anyway, how about you? How are your wedding plans coming along?
B Pretty good, thanks, but we still have a long ⁹_____ to go to get everything ready.
A Well, it goes without ¹⁰_____ that if there's anything I can do to help, you only have to ask!

PRONUNCIATION: /ə/ sound

5 ▶ 3.2 Read the sentences aloud, making sure you use the /ə/ sound in the parts in **bold**. Listen and repeat.

1 I prefer my soup to be a bit hott**er than** this.
2 They were climbing high**er and** high**er**.
3 **The** low**er** prices are, **the** more we can buy.
4 We'll have to get up **a** lot earlier **than** yesterday.
5 She's not nearly **as** interested in history **as** I am.

16

SKILLS 3D

SPEAKING: Reminiscing

1 ▶ 3.3 Listen to Keith and Bruno reminiscing about a bicycling trip. Match sentences 1–9 with a–i.

1 Do you remember that time _____
2 In retrospect, _____
3 Do you remember that family in Brattleboro _____
4 If I remember right, _____
5 It's all coming back to me now. _____
6 When I think back to some of the things we did, _____
7 With the benefit of hindsight, _____
8 When I look back on that summer, _____
9 If I could turn back time, _____

   a it just feels like a never-ending time of sunshine and freedom.
   b I'd do it all again, and do it just the same way!
   c We were so embarrassed, but they were really nice about it.
   d we certainly could have been better prepared!
   e that kindly helped us when you damaged your bike wheel?
   f it's amazing we didn't get into serious trouble.
   g we ended up camping in their backyard.
   h we biked from New York to Maine?
   i I think we could have done it a lot quicker.

2 ▶ 3.3 Listen again and complete these sentences in which the speakers fixed errors.

1 It took us about three days ... _____, didn't it?
2 And we accidentally set their bush on fire with our camping stove, _____ we had, didn't we?
3 And getting so, _____ on the way to that campsite on the Canadian border ...

3 Complete the conversations with phrases from exercise 1. There may be more than one correct answer, but do not use the same phrase twice.

A I loved having a big family. ¹_____ my childhood, I remember having a lot of fun.
B Oh, me, too! I loved hanging out with my four brothers.
A Although I do feel a bit sorry for my mom. ²_____, I can see that it must have been hard work for her. ³_____ I would probably try to help out a bit more.

A Why did you choose to study law?
B Good question! ⁴_____, I remember thinking that it would be exciting to take part in a trial and get justice for people. But ⁵_____, I don't think it was really the best subject for me.
A I thought it was because you met that lawyer on vacation, and you thought she was cool!
B Ah yes, ⁶_____. I think you're right!

4 Use your own ideas to complete the conversation.

A Do you remember that guy Jimmy who was in our class in high school?
B No, what did he look like?
A Well, if I remember right, _____.
B Oh, right, Jimmy Jukes. What a blast from the past! We were all pretty mean to him because of his funny accent, weren't we?
A Yes, we were. When I think back to that time, I feel _____. If I could turn back time, I'd _____.
B Yeah, kids can be so cruel. In retrospect, you realize _____. Do you know what happened to him?
A He went off to work on a cattle farm, you know, a dairy farm.
B Oh, yeah, it's all coming back to me now. And after that, he _____.
A That's right! So he did OK in the end. That's good. And we weren't mean to him all the time, were we?
B No, _____. Great times!

17

3 REVIEW and PRACTICE

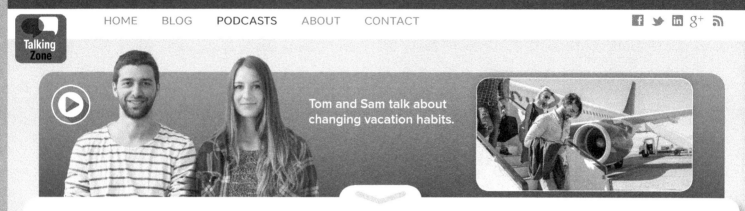

LISTENING

1 ▶ 3.4 Listen to Tom, Sam, and their guest talking about changes in our vacation habits. Check (✓) the points they discuss.

1 online travel services _____
2 the standard of beach houses _____
3 the problems with budget airlines _____
4 how to find your dream vacation _____
5 the changing role of travel agents _____
6 the differences between people of different ages _____
7 eating picnics on the beach _____
8 the increase in foreign travel _____

2 ▶ 3.4 Listen again and choose the correct options to complete the sentences.

1 Tom's grandma thinks she deserves an expensive vacation because she
  a is too old to stay in a cold beach house.
  b didn't enjoy her vacations when she was young.
  c hasn't had many adventures in her life.
2 John Lythgoe has written a book about
  a Darwin's theory of evolution.
  b how vacations have changed.
  c the history of beach houses.
3 Beach houses became nicer when
  a people started going to new vacation spots, instead.
  b people objected to cold water.
  c they were not comfortable enough.
4 Foreign vacations became more popular because
  a you could fly to the Caribbean.
  b people earned more, so they could afford them.
  c cheap flights became available.
5 John's company helps customers who
  a want to book a vacation online.
  b have problems trying to book their perfect vacation online.
  c want to make complicated travel arrangements.

READING

1 Read Sam's blog on page 19 and choose the best definition for the term "vintage clothing."
  a clothing that is for sale because the previous owner no longer wants it
  b clothing that is not new or modern, but is of good quality and can be worn today
  c old clothing that is valuable because of its historical interest

2 Choose the correct options to complete the sentences.

1 Sam thinks it is funny that she and her friends once liked _____ clothes.
  a different   b expensive   c similar
2 The sweatshirt she spent so much money on _____.
  a was soon ruined   b did not fit her
  c made her very happy
3 The dress Sam was wearing when she wrote the blog was made around _____ years ago.
  a 220   b 20   c 120
4 Her mother assumes she buys vintage clothes because new clothes are too _____.
  a boring   b expensive
  c poor in quality
5 The price of vintage clothing can be surprisingly _____.
  a high   b reasonable   c low
6 Sam thinks that _____ have had a negative effect on modern clothing.
  a changing fashions
  b financial considerations
  c global companies
7 It is _____ to alter vintage clothes than modern clothes to make them exactly the right size.
  a considerably harder
  b usually easier   c often more expensive
8 Sam says that vintage clothing is good if you _____ changing fashions.
  a are not concerned about
  b like to keep up with
  c worry about

18

REVIEW and PRACTICE 3

HOME BLOG PODCASTS ABOUT CONTACT

Sam writes about her love of vintage clothing.

Timeless fashion

Quite a lot of friends and acquaintances regard me as being a somewhat unconventional person in many respects, which, of course, I take as a compliment. This definitely applies to the clothes I choose to wear, and I'm proud to say that over the years, I've developed my own personal style.

When I was younger, I used to love going to the most popular clothing stores with my friends. It makes me laugh when I look at photos from that time because it seems that the more we spent, the more identical we looked! None of us were confident enough to develop our own style or risk any kind of creativity. And did I really save all my pocket money for three months to buy that designer sweatshirt that shrank the first time I washed it? Why did I ever think that was a good idea?

Well, as my friends know only too well, my tastes have undergone a radical change since then. No more chain stores for me! When it comes to fashion, it's vintage all the way! Nowadays, I adore spending weekend afternoons deep in the comfort of the city's many vintage clothing stores, searching for treasures from another era. Take the dress I'm wearing now: made at the turn of the twentieth century, the fabric is gorgeous, and the quality is far higher than you'll find in any contemporary clothing store.

My mom disapproves of my obsession, referring rather critically to my "second-hand" clothes, as if they're also somehow second-best. "Surely you can afford some new clothes now that you're working?" she says. "Why don't you get yourself something fashionable?" It goes without saying that I don't share her views. In fact, many of my clothes are a lot more expensive than she realizes – their price reflecting the demand for something unique, something with a history, something with a sense of mystery and romance.

And, as for being fashionable, well, I could tell her that good quality never goes out of fashion! Modern clothes are nowhere near as well-made because, these days, it's profit for the manufacturer that drives the decisions about how they're produced. You won't find a spare centimeter of fabric on a modern garment, whereas vintage clothes are generally extremely generous, a fact that means it's easy to make minor adjustments to them so that they fit perfectly. Also, in the past, dressmakers would add lovely details, such as the fabulous rose-shaped buttons on one of my vintage jackets. You don't find that kind of luxury now, without spending an absolute fortune.

Although it's the style and uniqueness of vintage clothes that attract me most, it's also nice to be able to give myself a pat on the back for helping to protect the environment. Every garment that's reused means that one less is made using the world's precious resources – in fact, probably several less, given the poor-quality, throwaway nature of much modern fashion. In addition, vintage clothes have given me the freedom to stop caring about the latest fashion trends, so if, like me, you've never been able to keep up, I'd recommend them as the perfect solution!

UNIT 4 Success and failure

4A — LANGUAGE

GRAMMAR: Verb patterns (1): infinitives and -ing forms

1 Complete the sentences with the words in the box.

> go going to go fix fixing
> to fix stay staying to stay

1 Do you remember _____ to Spain in 2015?
2 I need to get someone _____ my computer.
3 I don't mind _____ late to finish the work.
4 My boss made me _____ in a cheap hotel.
5 There's no point _____ the lawnmower. It's cheaper to buy a new one.
6 My parents wouldn't let me _____ on vacation with my friends.
7 Joe persuaded me _____ to yoga classes.
8 She's the first _____ in my apartment!
9 My brother helped me _____ the fence, which had blown down in the storm.

2 Find eight mistakes in the text. Cross out the mistakes and write the correct version above them.

Last year, I went to Mexico City on a five-day work trip. I had planned spending an extra day there at the end because I wanted to see the famous pyramids at Teotihuacán. As soon as I arrived, I asked the receptionist at the hotel to help me finding a day tour, and I signed up for one that looked fantastic. However, the day before the tour, I received a text. Apparently, I'd been the only person to sign up for that particular tour, so they'd been forced cancel it. I immediately started try to find a replacement tour, but I didn't really have enough time to do it, especially as I had meetings all day. Eventually, the receptionist advised me taking a private taxi, and that's what I did. We set off early the next morning so that we had plenty of time to look around. It was incredible. The pyramids were everything I'd hoped for. I will never forget to climb the biggest one. As I looked out across the Avenue of the Dead, it was easy to imagine people live their lives in this once great and powerful city. It was a truly amazing experience, and I would love going back there one day.

VOCABULARY: Success and failure

3 Complete the sentences with the words in the box.

> accomplished failed fulfilled thrived
> triumphed messed hold fell met went

1 My uncle's disability didn't _____ him back.
2 Last year I _____ my dream of learning to fly.
3 I'm afraid I _____ up on my math exam.
4 I'm very proud of what I've _____ this year.
5 The firm _____ bankrupt because of the recession.
6 My one attempt at humor _____ very flat.
7 He _____ over his critics by winning an Oscar.
8 His attempts to get rich all _____ miserably.
9 Last year she _____ her sales targets easily.
10 The company _____ under his leadership.

4 Complete the words in the sentences.

1 Sam p_____ his exam with f_____ c_____ .
2 Al was t_____ b_____ for the accident.
3 The show was superb. It e_____ my e_____ .
4 Her plan was very vague. It was l_____ i_____ detail.
5 The social media site was an amazing s_____ s_____ .
6 Nobody liked his idea. It went over like a l_____ b_____ .
7 If we don't hurry up, we'll m_____ the d_____ .
8 Her behavior f_____ s_____ of what we expected.

PRONUNCIATION: linking /w/ after to

5 ▶ 4.1 Read the sentences. Is there a sound you don't hear after to? Circle Y (Yes) or N (No). Listen, check, and repeat.

1 I really need something **to** drink. Y / N
2 She reminded me **to** take the garbage out. Y / N
3 He's always the first person **to** arrive in the morning. Y / N
4 I was forced **to** ask for help. Y / N
5 It's too hot **to** go outside. Y / N
6 We begged her **to** open the door. Y / N

SKILLS 4B

LISTENING: Understanding reasons and outcomes

1 ▶ 4.2 Listen to Ed telling Saskia about his naughty sister. Check (✓) the things he says.

1 Abby is usually well behaved. ____
2 She left the house without her parents' permission. ____
3 She was certain that her parents would look in her room. ____
4 She made it look as though she was asleep in her bed. ____
5 The dog tried to eat her hair. ____
6 Ed felt sorry for Abby. ____
7 Ed's mom has already thought of new punishments for her. ____
8 His parents wouldn't have been so mad about the vase if she'd been honest. ____
9 She had thrown away the broken pieces of vase. ____
10 She wasn't very good at hiding what she'd done. ____

2 ▶ 4.2 Listen again and fill in the blanks in these sentences from the conversation.

1 She'd been prevented from going out _____ something she did last week.
2 She knew our parents were _____ suspicious _____ they'd be bound to check up on her.
3 And, _____, she's in even more trouble than she was before!
4 _____, he was even angrier than he would have been if she'd told the truth.

3 Complete the sentences with the correct form of the verbs in parentheses.

1 If Marco had apologized, his mother _____ so angry. (be)
2 I would have come to your party if you _____ me. (invite)
3 If I hadn't lost my phone, we _____ to call you. (be able)
4 The child could have died if we _____ her cries. (hear)
5 If I'd realized you didn't know her, I _____ you. (introduce)

4 ▶ 4.3 Look at these sentences. Use the mark ‿ to show links between consonants and vowels, consonants and consonants, and vowels and vowels. Listen and check.

1 Abby wasn't allowed to go out.
2 Abby wanted to go out to the party.
3 The dog ran out of Abby's room.
4 Ed heard his mother's scream.
5 Mom wants Abby to do some jobs around the house.
6 She broke the vase by accident.
7 Dad discovered the pieces of vase.
8 They knew it was Abby who'd broken the antique vase.

5 Match sentences 1–6 with a–f.

1 Harry wasn't too upset when I told him I'd broken his headphones. ____
2 I feel that Joe should have been a bit more grateful for our help. ____
3 Carlos didn't do enough studying when he was in college. ____
4 Peter ended up on the wrong side of town. ____
5 Adam was upset when she said she thought they should split up. ____
6 Sam earned just enough to live on. ____

a He should have made more time for it.
b He took it very badly.
c He took it for granted.
d He managed to make ends meet.
e He took it well.
f He took a wrong turn.

21

4C — LANGUAGE

GRAMMAR: Adding emphasis (2): inversion and *do/does/did*

1 Complete the sentences with the verb phrases in the box.

> does she regret   she did steal   I do see
> she does regret   had we started
> we did start   did she steal   have I seen

1 Scarcely _____ eating than we were told to go back to work.
2 Not only _____ the money, but she also lied about it afterwards.
3 Seldom _____ so many lions in one place.
4 She's happy living in Rome, but _____ leaving her friends behind.
5 María has just admitted that _____ my necklace.
6 It's true that we left work after lunch on Thursday, but _____ early on Friday morning.
7 I've lost touch with most of my high school friends, but _____ Cameron now and then.
8 Only when she's particularly tired _____ becoming a doctor.

2 Complete the sentences with the words in parentheses. They are not always given in the correct order. Use the correct form of the verbs.

1 The painting must have been worth millions. _____ such a valuable painting in a private house. (come across / I / rarely)
2 _____ why my father was often so unhappy. (understand / only now / I)
3 _____ new regulations in advance. (hardly ever / they / announce)
4 Sara showed me the letter. _____ why she had decided to leave. (become / clear / only then / it)
5 Freddie told his dad he was studying, but _____ than he started playing video games. (no sooner / his father / leave)
6 I knew I had hurt my leg, but _____ how badly I had cut it. (get undressed / I / realize / not until / I)
7 She is very stressed, but _____ her rudeness. (excuse / that / in no way)
8 These men are dangerous. _____ to enter the area. (on no account / be allowed / they / should)

VOCABULARY: Idioms

3 Choose the correct options to complete the sentences.

1 After six months they realized that they had *let their hair down / bitten off more than they could chew*, and that now there was too much work for two people.
2 *It costs an arm and a leg / You bite off more than you can chew* when you have dinner at that hotel.
3 She's normally so serious when she's at work, but at the party on Saturday, she really *called it a day / let her hair down*.
4 The news that they were getting married *was the last straw / came out of the blue*. We hadn't expected it.
5 There was still work to do, but everyone was tired, so we decided to *call it a day / fight a losing battle*.
6 My grandpa had a great sense of humor. He was always *hitting the nail on the head / pulling my leg*.
7 Thank you for all your suggestions. You've definitely given us *a piece of cake / food for thought*.
8 Not getting a pay raise was *a blessing in disguise / the last straw*. She began to look for a new job.

4 Complete the words in the sentences.

1 People in my office sometimes use the photocopier for personal documents, but our boss usually turns a b_____ eye.
2 I have the best of both w_____ because my apartment gives me independence, but my family is still nearby.
3 Losing my old job was a b_____ in disguise because now I'm doing something I really love.
4 He really hit the n_____ on the head when he described the minister as "a man with no shame."
5 Take Jo with you. She knows the area i_____ out.
6 We're bound to face opposition from local people, but we'll cross that b_____ when we come to it.
7 I'm trying to keep my garden in order, but I sometimes feel I'm fighting a l_____ battle.

PRONUNCIATION: Sentence stress: emphatic *do/does/did*

5 ▶ 4.4 Read the sentences aloud, remembering to stress *do, does,* or *did*. Listen and repeat.

1 Unfortunately, I think your dog **does** have something wrong with his heart.
2 I know it wasn't your intention, but that joke **did** upset me.
3 **Do** sit down and have a cup of coffee.
4 Although she denies it, Hannah **did** cheat on her exam.
5 It's true that our computer system **does** have some problems.

22

SKILLS 4D

Writing: Writing a report

1 Read the report and complete the text with the linkers in the box. There may be more than one correct answer, but do not use the same linker twice.

due to	since	as a result	therefore
consequently	in order to	so as to	nevertheless
nonetheless	in addition	moreover	furthermore

Annual Report of the

Castle Road Club

A Introduction
The Castle Road Club was established a year ago ¹_____ enable residents of Castle Road to get to know one another and to create a greater sense of community. The aim of this report is to evaluate the program's first year and make suggestions for developing it over the following 12 months.

B Achievements
Residents of over 20 households attended an initial meeting to discuss the project. Letters were then delivered to every house ²_____ make all residents aware of the club. ³_____, more than 50 people signed up on our Facebook page, and it was agreed we would have a block party in June. This was an extremely successful event, with more than 150 people attending. ⁴_____, three new groups were formed: a book group, a babysitting circle, and a jogging group.

C Challenges
The Castle Road Club has undoubtedly led to an increase in community spirit. ⁵_____, a significant number of residents have not taken part ⁶_____ a range of issues, such as work commitments or disability. ⁷_____, several residents in the 18–25 age range report a lack of interest in the groups currently being offered. Suggestions have been made for additional groups, but it has been difficult to find people willing to take responsibility for them, and ⁸_____ no further groups have been set up.

D Recommendations
I recommend that we form a small committee to look into these issues, and I will be looking for volunteers for this task. ⁹_____, I propose sending a questionnaire to all households to ask for feedback on the club and suggestions for future activities. ¹⁰_____ the last block party was so successful, I have already applied to the city to close the road on June 17th for a similar event this year.

Gemma Kennedy
Chair, Castle Road Club

2 Rewrite these informal sentences to make them appropriate for a formal report.

1 We managed to get over 40 people to join our club.
_____

2 Unfortunately, our New Year's Day event was a bit of a disaster.
_____

3 This report is about all the things that were good or bad over the last year.
_____

4 Members keep arguing about the club rules.
_____

5 This report lets you know how the club did this year.
_____

6 We probably need to get better at letting people know what's going on.
_____

7 Most people thought the activities we organized were great.
_____

8 We need to do something to get more members.
_____

3 Look at the sentences in exercise 2. Write sentence numbers 1–8 next to the paragraph in which they are most likely to appear (A–D).

A Introduction _____ _____
B Progress/Achievements _____ _____
C Difficulties/Challenges _____ _____
D Future developments/Recommendations _____ _____

4 Complete the sentences with your own ideas.

1 We have faced challenges finding qualified instructors. Nevertheless, _____.

2 We have lost almost half of our membership in the last three months. Consequently, _____.

3 We have produced a short booklet about the community center. In addition, _____.

4 We have introduced a small membership fee in order to _____.

5 Our last two meetings had to be canceled due to _____.

5 Imagine you have started one of the following clubs. Write an annual report describing its first year. You should structure your report using the paragraph types referred to in exercise 3.

a karate club   a chess club   a music group
a cooking club   a local history society

23

4 REVIEW and PRACTICE

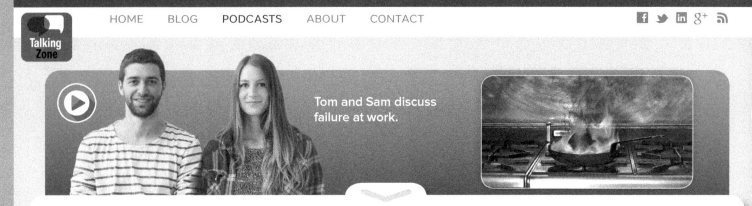

LISTENING

1 ▶ 4.5 Listen to the podcast and number a–f in the order that you hear them (1–6).

a Tom's job with the fire department ____
b how Sam felt after her job with children ____
c their job making podcasts ____
d what they thought of the comedian's own show ____
e Sam's job with children ____
f the reaction of their listeners to the podcast with the comedian ____

2 ▶ 4.5 Listen again and choose the correct options to complete the sentences.

1 Making podcasts is
 a something you can only do if you are lucky.
 b something most people would be good at.
 c not particularly difficult.
2 When Tom and Sam invited a comedian to take part in their podcast,
 a his type of humor did not work well.
 b he was extremely funny.
 c he ruined all his jokes.
3 They were surprised about this because
 a his humor was similar to theirs.
 b he was an experienced performer.
 c his own show was very funny.
4 When Sam worked with young children, her boss
 a tried to make her keep control.
 b usually ignored what was going on.
 c had to apologize to the angry parents.
5 That job made Sam
 a doubt her own abilities.
 b certain that she never wanted to work with children again.
 c think that working with children was easy.
6 When Tom was a new firefighter, he
 a was so nervous, he was sick.
 b did things that showed he wasn't appropriate for the job.
 c caused a fire that badly damaged the kitchen of the firehouse.

READING

1 Read Tom's blog on page 25 about training for a marathon and choose the best summary.

a Tom's marathon training schedule has not been going well, so his mother told him to read about other people who have achieved difficult things. Finding out about how proud they felt when they achieved them has inspired him to start training again.
b Tom's mother suggested reading about other big challenges in order to encourage him to train for his marathon. This turned out to be a bad idea because he discovered that people often do not get pleasure from achieving their goals.
c Tom has been finding it difficult to keep training for his marathon, so he read about people who achieved great things in order to try and motivate himself. He discovered that their sense of pride and achievement often came some time after they had fulfilled their goal.

2 Are the sentences true (T), false (F), or doesn't say (DS)?

1 Tom has been considering running a marathon for a long time. ____
2 He is worried that it might be too difficult for him. ____
3 His mom thinks he should give up the idea. ____
4 The Everest climbers had only negative feelings when they completed their climb. ____
5 Coming down from Everest is more dangerous than going up. ____
6 Michael Collins felt very proud when his colleagues walked on the moon. ____
7 He was completely confident they would get back to the command module safely. ____
8 Ben Saunders' experience fulfilling an ambition was similar to that of the climbers and astronauts. ____
9 The moment he achieved his goal, he felt a sense of triumph. ____
10 Tom thinks that running a marathon is something he will be very proud of. ____

HOME   BLOG   PODCASTS   ABOUT   CONTACT

Tom writes about fulfilling ambitions.

What an achievement!

As some of you know, I'm running a marathon in October. It's something I've always wanted to do, but there has always been something holding me back (mainly my own laziness!). Anyway, earlier this year, I decided that it was time to stop talking about it and just get on with it, so I went online, got myself one of those "couch to marathon" planners and started training.

At first, I did stick to my plan, but recently I seem to have lost motivation, and I was worried that I may have bitten off more than I can chew. When it's time for my run, I always seem to find some other urgent task to do (like straightening up my sock drawer or arranging my books in alphabetical order!). My mom advised me to read about people who have achieved amazing things, because she thought that might provide enough inspiration to get me going again.

Initially, it seemed like very poor advice. I started with people who had climbed Everest, and while some of them mentioned the beauty of the scenery or their sense of relief at having reached the summit, their overwhelming emotion seemed to be fear of the dangers still ahead. They were only too aware that the descent would be as hazardous as the ascent, at a time when they were already physically exhausted. Not until they had reached the comparative safety of their base camp were they able to take pleasure in what they had accomplished.

Similarly, Michael Collins, the third member of the Apollo 11 crew, admits that after watching his colleagues Neil Armstrong and Buzz Aldrin complete their historic moon walk, there was no time for congratulations because there was still so much work to do, including a tense operation to return their small lunar module to the larger command module where he was waiting for them. In fact, he had already prepared a speech about their heroism in case they didn't make it.

By the time I started reading about Ben Saunders, who undertook a 105-day trek to the South Pole, I was beginning to see a pattern emerge. Saunders had triumphed over exhaustion and extreme weather conditions to complete the journey (which, by the way, was the equivalent of 69 marathons back-to-back, putting my feeble efforts into perspective!), but only when he was safe, warm, and well fed again was he able to enjoy his achievement.

So perhaps my mother does have a point. I may not be guaranteed an incredible sense of satisfaction at the finish line, but I can probably expect it to come later. It may not be much compared to walking on the moon, but it will mean a lot to me. OK, I'd better go and get my running shoes on!

UNIT 5 Entertain us!

5A LANGUAGE

GRAMMAR: Ellipsis and substitution

1 Cross out any words that can be omitted in each sentence without changing its meaning.

1 You can come with us if you'd like, but you don't have to come with us.
2 They went to John's house and they had a barbecue.
3 I've never swum a mile, but I think I could swim a mile.
4 She says she didn't write the letter, but I think she did write it.
5 Jamie said the exam was hard, but it wasn't hard.
6 I asked Jo to invite Tom, but she won't invite him.
7 Would you like to go for a walk or would you like to watch a movie?
8 Amy might bring some sandwiches, but if she doesn't bring any, we'll still have enough food.

2 Complete the conversation with the words in the box.

to   ones   so (x3)   not   one (x2)   is   will

A Do you think Susie will like her birthday present?
B Yes, I hope ¹_____. It's a beautiful necklace. I have ²_____ that's very similar, and I wear it a lot.
A Does Susie often wear jewelry?
B Yes, she does. And she loves silver. She has lots of silver earrings. Have you seen the ³_____ that are shaped like leaves?
A I think ⁴_____. She was wearing them at Helen's barbecue, wasn't she? Is the necklace we're giving her real silver?
B Well, it says ⁵_____ on the box, so I hope it ⁶_____. If ⁷_____, we've wasted our money!
A Are you planning to wear a dress to her party?
B Yes, I think I ⁸_____. I need to buy ⁹_____. Do you want to come and help me choose it?
A Of course. I'd love ¹⁰_____!

VOCABULARY: Tastes and opinions

3 Choose the correct options to complete the sentences.

1 I've never been a *wild / huge / strong* fan of science fiction.
2 The play had some good parts, but I wouldn't rate it more than *average / outstanding / appalling*.
3 The idea of swimming with dolphins doesn't really *adore / desire / appeal to* me.
4 Steven Spielberg is my favorite movie director. I *detest / despise / adore* all his films.
5 The continual sound of pop music began to *get / be / have* on my nerves.
6 Have you seen this video game? All the kids are *strong / wild / huge* about it.
7 The movie got really bad reviews. It was really *inadequate / appalling / outstanding*.
8 No oysters for me, thanks. I *appeal to / detest / adore* seafood.

4 Complete the words.

1 This hotel is nowhere near as good as the last one. Everything about it is in_____or.
2 I have never seen such dramatic scenery. It was absolutely s_____ar!
3 We spent most of our time in the next town, on the coast. We found it p_____able to where we were staying.
4 She just said the same thing over and over in different ways. It was such a t_____ous lecture.
5 She was wearing a gorgeous dress, and she'd had her hair done. She looked f_____ous.
6 I've never had a student as good as Lewis. He really was ex_____al.
7 The facilities were totally in_____ate for so many people. There were only two showers!
8 We absolutely loved the circus, and the acrobats were s_____al. I've never seen such a thrilling performance.
9 My brother plays video games all day long, He's completely o_____ed with them.
10 The new medication needs further testing, but scientists are happy with the initial results, which look very p_____ing.

PRONUNCIATION: Strong and weak forms of *to*

5 ▶5.1 Read the sentences aloud. Pay attention to the pronunciation of *to*. Listen and repeat.

1 We'd been hoping **to** rent a car, but we couldn't afford **to**.
2 I wanted **to** go in the building, but I wasn't allowed **to**.
3 It's best not **to** take any medication unless you really have **to**.
4 I have **to** iron, even though I don't want **to**.
5 I had enough money **to** take a cab, but I decided not **to**.

26

READING: Understanding tone

New Year, New You! Sandy Mason

Just what the world needs – another self-help book claiming it can turn you into the rich, popular, and glamorous person you've always wanted to be. As a poor, but contented introvert who likes nothing better than curling up alone with a book, it's fair to say that I'm not exactly Sandy Mason's target audience. Nevertheless, I tried to keep an open mind as I struggled through chapters such as "Dress for success" (No, thanks, I like my jeans) or "Social media for social success" (I only post cute pictures of my cats). Even the chapters that sounded useful, such as "Think yourself rich" – and who couldn't do with a bit more cash? – turned out to be a series of slogans with almost no content. New Year, Same old, same old!

Digging for the Planet Tristram Hughes

Numerous TV appearances have made Tristram Hughes a household name. His enthusiastic gardening advice coupled with a dry and sometimes wicked sense of humor mean he is a firm favorite with gardeners everywhere. In this, his fifth book, he goes back to basics. Twenty beautifully illustrated chapters cover everything you need to know about growing your own food. Whether you garden in a field or a window box, Hughes' message is that this is the best thing you can do for the environment. And although this is what he is most passionate about, he achieves the difficult task of leaving his readers feeling entertained, (much!) better informed, but never lectured at.

Muck and Magic: Memories of an Iowa Farm Jack Leeson

Although Jack Leeson's family has been farming the same fertile Iowa fields for six generations, Jack himself was tempted by the bright lights of New York, where he started his highly successful club, JL Nights. On the basis of this memoir, he should probably stick to the day (or rather, night) job. Although he clearly has a great affection for his family home, Leeson fundamentally has nothing of interest to say about it. Milk yields rise and fall; his dad buys a new tractor; an extended dry spell threatens the wheat crop. Who cares? In the hands of a more gifted writer, this might not matter, but Leeson's prose is the literary equivalent of being given a stale crust of bread when you were hoping for a cheesecake.

1 Read these reviews by the critic Michael Forth. Does he say these things? Circle Y (Yes) or N (No).

1. He enjoys spending his free time on his own. Y / N
2. Sandy Mason's book is aimed at people like him. Y / N
3. He tried to follow the advice in her book. Y / N
4. He would like to have more money. Y / N
5. Tristram Hughes is very popular. Y / N
6. He says you can grow food even if you don't have much space. Y / N
7. His book makes you feel guilty if you buy food in grocery stores. Y / N
8. Jack Leeson left the family farm when he was a teenager. Y / N
9. His book describes ordinary farm life. Y / N
10. Leeson's writing style does not engage the reader. Y / N

2 Which of the adjectives in the box could you use to describe the tone of each review? Write them in the correct column. Some adjectives may go in more than one column.

admiring   critical   informative   bored
unimpressed   humorous   serious
sarcastic   disappointed

New Year, New You!	Digging for the Planet	Muck and Magic: Memories of an Iowa Farm
_____	_____	_____
_____	_____	_____
_____	_____	_____
_____	_____	_____

3 Circle the subject in the first four sentences of the first review. Then circle the subjects in the sentences below.

1. Even though she had never met Alfonso's younger brother before, and everyone had told her how shy he was, Lucia was determined to include him on their trip to the mountains.
2. To Greg's horror, particularly because he knew how valuable it was, and how much his aunt loved it, the vase now had a large crack from top to bottom.
3. The train, which had been due to arrive in Miami earlier that morning, had been delayed by heavy snow overnight in the northeast.
4. If you include all the time we spent preparing our classes and traveling to and from the site, the fee we received for teaching the course was not generous at all.

5C LANGUAGE

GRAMMAR: Noun phrases

1 Complete the noun phrases in the sentences below with the words in the box. Then <u>underline</u> the complete noun phrase.

> opinion gallery entrance
> cousin's bike set son water
> boots paintings woman Paul's
> plates office matter pair

1 I wish we'd listened to the advice of the _____ who told us to bring plenty of _____ .

2 Meet me at the _____ of the doctor's _____ .

3 I've never met _____ oldest _____ .

4 This is one of the _____ previously kept at the _____ in Moscow.

5 They gave me an incredibly expensive _____ of dinner _____ .

6 Have you seen Billy's _____ new racing _____ ?

7 I want to buy a _____ of leather walking _____ .

8 To me, Kelvin has a completely different _____ on the _____ .

2 Are the noun phrases in these sentences correct or incorrect? Cross out any mistakes and write the correct noun phrases at the end of the sentences.

1 They sell great burgers including vegetarian very tasty ones. _____

2 He's one of my old colleagues from the supermarket. _____

3 We're inviting our whole from Italy family to the wedding. _____

4 That is the biggest I've ever seen cat! _____

5 The most beautiful place I know is a small sandy beach in northern France. _____

6 Why don't you have a cold nice drink of orange freshly-squeezed juice? _____

7 Where should I put my case of guitar? _____

8 They live in a wooden rather old-fashioned house in the center of Atlanta. _____

VOCABULARY: Verb suffixes

3 Choose the correct options to complete the sentences.

1 You could add some honey to *ripen / emphasize / sweeten* the apples.

2 You can't really *generalize / summarize / specify* about all people from the U.S.

3 She's going to wear braces to *soften / justify / straighten* her teeth.

4 The government refuses to *brighten / negotiate / notify* with terrorists.

5 He said he wanted a newspaper, but he didn't *anticipate / simplify / specify* which one.

6 Take the butter out of the fridge so that it *softens / brightens / ripens* a bit.

7 You will be *summarized / notified / negotiated* when the test results are ready.

8 I want to *emphasize / simplify / summarize* how important it is to wear a helmet.

4 Complete the verbs in the box and use them to complete the second sentence so that it means the same as the first sentence.

> associ_____ exagger_____ deterior_____ weak_____
> sympath_____ clari_____ minim_____ bright_____

1 I hope that this document will make the procedure clear.
I hope that this document will _____ .

2 I admit that when I described my injuries, I pretended that they were worse than they really were.
I admit that I _____ .

3 She was upset about having to work late, and I felt sorry for her.
She was upset about having to work late, and I _____ .

4 I felt that he was trying to say that my problems weren't important.
I felt that he was trying to _____ .

5 A few lamps would help to make the room lighter.
A few lamps would help to _____ .

6 The quality of the food has gotten worse over the last year.
The quality of the food has _____ .

7 When I see the ocean, I always think of Jim.
I always _____ with Jim.

8 If you add too much water, it will make the flavor less strong.
If you add too much water, it will _____ .

PRONUNCIATION: Word stress in compound nouns

5 ▶ 5.2 Read the sentences aloud and <u>underline</u> the stressed syllable in the compound nouns in **bold**. Listen and check.

1 Natalie can stay in the **guest room**.

2 My **mouse mat** has a picture of an elephant on it.

3 I had to go to the **eye doctor**.

4 Don't forget to put on plenty of **sunscreen**.

5 They have a **guard dog** to protect their house.

6 I never use my phone at the **dinner table**.

SKILLS 5D

SPEAKING: Speculating

1 ▶ 5.3 Listen to Charlie and Faye discussing a musical Charlie is directing. Match 1–12 with a–l.

1 I suppose … _____
2 I wouldn't be surprised if … _____
3 That can't be … _____
4 Chances are that … _____
5 It's unlikely that … _____
6 In all probability … _____
7 My guess is … _____
8 I wonder whether … _____
9 I assume … _____
10 I doubt … _____
11 It must be … _____
12 I bet … _____

   a around 45.
   b it will be great.
   c we'll end up taking a loss.
   d she'll be very good.
   e we'll sell more than around 80 tickets.
   f you have Chloe Latimer in the lead role?
   g difficult for her, coming in at this late stage.
   h we'll lose some more.
   i easy.
   j I could persuade some of my friends to come.
   k there's a lot to do?
   l I end up forgetting something critical.

2 ▶ 5.3 Listen again. Match the examples of repetition 1–5 to functions a–e.

1 Barbara Ratcliffe? _____
2 So far? _____
3 *Mamma Mia*? _____
4 Chloe Latimer? _____
5 August 4th? _____

   a to clarify something that has been said
   b to correct something that someone has said
   c to show interest in something that has been said
   d to show surprise about something
   e to give someone time to think before he/she responds

3 Complete the conversation with phrases from exercise 1. There may be more than one correct answer.

Alice Hey, Lucas! How's drama school? ¹_____ you must be in your last year now?
Lucas My last year? No, actually, I finished in July. I'm just on my way to try out for a part in a movie that's being made here. ²_____ I'll get it, though. ³_____ there will be hundreds of people going for it.
Alice Hundreds? Well, ⁴_____ you get it, anyway. I remember you in the school plays we used to have, and you were fantastic!
Lucas Thanks, Alice! Well, even if I don't get that part, ⁵_____ that they'll have other, smaller parts they need to fill.
Alice Sure. ⁶_____ any part is better than no part at this stage in your career.
Lucas That's right. ⁷_____ it's best to take whatever I can get at the moment.
Alice Yes, but you also need to be confident. Go for it, Lucas! ⁸_____ you'll get the part!

4 Write a short conversation between two friends discussing a show they're taking part in. Use phrases from exercise 1 and repetition for some of the functions in exercise 2.

_____
_____
_____
_____
_____

29

5 REVIEW and PRACTICE

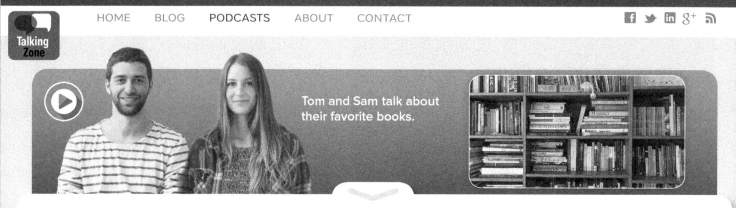

LISTENING

1 ▶ 5.4 Listen to Tom and Sam talking about the books they like. Complete the sentences with one word.

1. Tom doesn't enjoy reading _____.
2. Sam says that our _____ work in similar ways when we read fiction as when we interact with other people.
3. Sam thinks non-fiction books are _____.
4. Tom has recently read a book about _____.
5. Tom says that _____ are as interesting as novels.
6. He thinks that Sam needs to learn more about _____.

2 ▶ 5.4 Listen again. Are the sentences true (T), false (F), or doesn't say (DS)?

1. Tom thinks that Sam usually reads poor-quality books. ____
2. Sam is currently reading a non-fiction book. ____
3. Tom likes to learn things while he is reading. ____
4. Tom hasn't read any books about neuroscience. ____
5. Reading fiction helps us have better personal relationships. ____
6. It is easier to understand characters in a book than people in real life. ____
7. Tom was inspired to read non-fiction by the textbooks he had in school. ____
8. It is difficult to find non-fiction books that are well-written. ____
9. Biographies teach more about history than conventional history books. ____
10. Sam and Tom agree to choose a book for the other to read. ____

READING

1 Read Sam's blog on page 31 and choose the best summary.

a. Sam went to a performance-art event with her friend Jack. She didn't tell him how bored she was and, afterwards, tried to appear interested as he described two other performance art events to her. Although she thought they sounded boring, she understands why he found them interesting.

b. Sam and Jack watched a performance that involved painting. Later, Jack described some other performance-art events to Sam. She thought they sounded more interesting than the one they saw, but was still not eager to go to them.

c. Jack is interested in performance art and invited Sam to a performance-art event. She found it boring and didn't think the other pieces of performance art Jack described to her afterwards sounded interesting, either.

2 Does Sam say these things in her blog? Circle Y (Yes) or N (No).

1. She didn't realize she was going to a performance art event. Y / N
2. The artist they saw painted himself as part of the performance. Y / N
3. He kept painting throughout the entire performance. Y / N
4. Jack enjoys trying to figure out the meaning of performance-art events. Y / N
5. She disagreed with Jack about the meaning of what they had seen. Y / N
6. Jack told her about a work designed to make people think differently about time. Y / N
7. Several people who were sitting at the same table as the artist were so bored that they cried. Y / N
8. In the event "The Maybe," an actress and an artist took turns sitting in a glass box. Y / N
9. She wouldn't be satisfied if she saw "The Maybe" with nobody in the box. Y / N
10. She doesn't have particularly fixed ideas about what art should be. Y / N

REVIEW and PRACTICE 5

HOME　　BLOG　　PODCASTS　　ABOUT　　CONTACT

Sam writes about performance art.

But what's the point?

It's always nice to do something a bit different on the weekend, after working away all week. Saturday night is when I tend to go out with my friends, and it's usually the highlight of our week. We might go to the movies, to a concert, or to someone's house for a party. But this Saturday didn't exactly live up to my expectations ...

Ever felt like watching paint dry? Me neither, but that's exactly what I did on Saturday evening. My friend Jack invited me to this thing at the gallery where he works. I'd assumed it was a play, but it turned out to be a piece of so-called "performance art." Well, before last Saturday, I didn't even know such a thing existed, and although I know I shouldn't generalize on the basis of one experience, I have to say I have no desire to sit through anything like that ever again.

To summarize, a man wearing a swimsuit strolled onto the stage and opened four pots of vividly-colored paint. He then painted some random patches on the floor and some stripes down his own body. And, um ... that was about it. After that, he just sat on the floor and stared at what he'd painted for half an hour. I don't think I'd be exaggerating to say that it was one of the most tedious things I've ever seen – certainly the most tedious thing I've ever *paid* to see!

Incredibly, Jack claimed that he'd enjoyed it. He says that what appeals to him about performance art is the relationship with the audience: the fact that our reaction is an essential part of it. He says that it stretches you intellectually because you are forced to draw your own conclusions about the meaning of the work, rather than taking a passive role. However, when I asked him to specify the conclusions he'd drawn about what we'd just seen, he was vague, to say the least!

Over pizza later on, he told me about several famous performance-art events, such as one where an artist sat silently at a table for eight hours a day for almost three months, while spectators took turns sitting across from her and staring into her eyes. The idea was that extending the

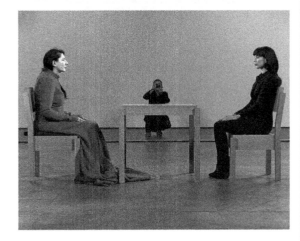

performance beyond a normal length of time was supposed to alter viewers' perception of time and deepen their experience. Apparently, some people were moved to tears by it. (Tears of boredom, probably, I thought.)

Then there was the one where an actress slept in a glass box – but only sometimes! The "piece" was called "The Maybe" (as in "maybe you'll see me, maybe you won't," I guess). She and the artist she collaborated with justified that potential for disappointment by explaining that uncertainty was part of the concept. Personally, I can't imagine being anything other than fed-up if I'd gone all the way to a gallery to see an empty glass box, but perhaps that's just my lack of imagination.

Clearly, Jack finds all this kind of stuff fascinating, but, frankly, I just don't get it. I'm pretty open-minded when it comes to art. I'm certainly not like those people who dismiss a painting if they "can't tell what it's supposed to be," but, despite all his efforts to educate me, I don't think I'll ever be able to find watching paint dry any more interesting than, well ... watching paint dry!

31

WRITING PRACTICE

WRITING: Giving constructive criticism

1 Read the text. <u>Underline</u> the two phrases that Lucy uses to introduce negative points in order to sound more polite.

> Hi Sophie!
>
> It was really good to see you last week. It's been far too long, and we had a lot of catching up to do!
>
> I've been thinking about you these past few days, and I'd like to pass on a few thoughts. They may be of no use at all, in which case feel free to ignore everything I say! I just hate to think about there being so much bad feeling in your family. You've always been so close.
>
> First of all, I *do* understand why you're unhappy with your brother's behavior. He's still behaving like the baby of the family, demanding help from his parents (and big sister!) whenever life gets tough. I would agree that, at 28, this is pretty ridiculous. But I think that you should try to tackle the issue with your brother yourself, rather than getting mad at your parents. You reported having a conversation in which you were [1]**quite** angry with them. I hope you don't mind me saying this, but I'm not [2]**quite** sure that blaming your (very nice!) mom and dad for your brother's adult behavior will help. It might make things awkward between you and your parents while serving no real purpose.
>
> The other thing that bothered me was what you said about your childhood. You say that your brother was your parents' favorite child, and this makes you feel [3]**quite** bitter. Please don't think that I'm judging you, but I don't [4]**quite** know why the things that happened to you while you were growing up still bother you so much. It's all now in the past. You have such a full and successful life, Sophie. Try not to let your feelings about your childhood affect you now. As adults, we have to take responsibility for our own happiness.
>
> I'm sorry if I sound a little impatient, Sophie, but I think we all need a "critical friend" from time to time. I hope very much that you'll give me constructive advice, too, when I need it ...
>
> Love, Lucy xxx

2 Lucy is critical of certain aspects of Sophie's character and behavior. Check (✔) the aspects that she mentions.

1 Sophie treats her brother badly. _____

2 She gets angry with her parents. _____

3 She doesn't think enough about other people. _____

4 She thinks too much about the unpleasant things in her past. _____

5 She lets her anger spoil her otherwise very good life. _____

3 Read the text again and find examples of the following.

1 an acceptance by Lucy that there is a problem

_____

2 two positive points that Lucy makes in order to balance the negative ones

_____

_____

3 a reference to a specific thing that Sophie did that Lucy disapproves of

_____

4 a recommendation for improving the situation

_____

4 Look at the four examples (1–4) of *quite* in the e-mail. How are they being used?

a before an adjective of degree, meaning *pretty* or *fairly* _____

b in a phrase that "softens" a negative opinion _____

5 Think about a person you know who is doing something that you disapprove of. Write a helpful e-mail to them offering constructive criticism.

- Be encouraging by including positive points as well as negative ones.

- Introduce your criticisms with "softening" phrases so that you don't sound rude.

- Avoid phrases that are extreme or very direct.

- Give at least one specific example of the thing that you disapprove of.

- Make at least one positive suggestion for improving the thing that you are criticizing.

WRITING PRACTICE

WRITING: Writing a report

Report on the introduction of the new IT system at Fuller and Morris, Inc. *Paul Greenwood, IT Director*

A _____

Unfortunately, we have encountered a few issues with incorrect data being input, due to confusion over the wording on some of the input screens. Consequently, some errors were made when supplying orders to customers, although these were quickly corrected, and no lasting damage was done to the reputation of the company.

B _____

In May of last year, we implemented our new IT system. This followed a year-long development phase and extensive consultation with staff in order to ensure that it would meet the needs of every department. The purpose of this report is to evaluate that implementation and to assess the performance of the new system after its first year in operation.

C _____

I recommend that we work with staff to improve on-screen instructions so as to eliminate data-entry errors. In addition, we will be holding extra training sessions for users who feel they would benefit from them. To sum up, the system has been extremely successful. Nevertheless, I recommend that we continue to monitor performance and encourage staff members to suggest ideas for further improvement.

D _____

First, I would like to thank all staff members who contributed to development and testing. Their work was invaluable to the IT team. As a result, we were able to design a system that has enabled us all to work more efficiently and has, therefore, increased productivity. Furthermore, our recent staff survey showed a high level of satisfaction with the system.

---

1 Read the report and number paragraphs A–D in the correct order 1–4.

1 _____ 2 _____ 3 _____ 4 _____

2 Choose the correct heading for each paragraph.

1 Recommendations for the future
2 What went well?
3 Introduction
4 What were our challenges?

3 <u>Underline</u> the formal words and phrases in the text that could be used to replace the informal phrases in **bold** in these sentences.

1 We have **had** problems with the new equipment. (paragraph A)
2 We installed the new equipment after **asking staff members what they thought**. (paragraph B)
3 The purpose of this report is to **see how successful** the new machinery **has been**. (paragraph B)
4 We will be arranging training in order to stop these mistakes **from happening**. (paragraph C)
5 We will continue to **see how performance is doing**. (paragraph C)
6 We'd like staff to **tell us how we can make things better**. (paragraph C)
7 Many staff members **helped with** the development of our new product range. (paragraph D)
8 Feedback from staff members shows **that they really like** the new offices. (paragraph D)

4 Using the linkers in the box, match 1–8 to a–h. There may be more than one correct answer.

> nevertheless   as a result   since   furthermore
> moreover   due to   in order to   therefore

1 Our existing customers were very pleased and, _____,
2 Our new offices are bigger and, _____,
3 The move to Philadelphia was _____
4 Staff members were able to use the new equipment safely _____
5 We listened closely to the views of our staff and, _____,
6 We took on some more staff _____
7 Staff members were offered a good relocation package but, _____,
8 The new machinery is easier to operate and, _____,

  a they had all taken training courses.
  b more pleasant to work in.
  c many of them chose to leave the company.
  d large rent increases for office space in New York.
  e cope with the increase in demand.
  f we attracted orders from new customers.
  g the quality of our products has improved.
  h made several changes to the plan.

5 Write a fictional report about a major change within a company. Use one of the ideas in the box or your own idea.

> moving a company to a new city/country
> introducing new equipment, e.g., robots
> starting to make a new product

- Include an introduction.
- Describe what went well and the reasons.
- Describe what didn't go as well and the reasons.
- Make recommendations for the future.

63

Richmond

58 St Aldates
Oxford
OX1 1ST
United Kingdom

ISBN: 978-84-668-2554-2
© Richmond / Santillana Global S.L. 2019

Publishing Director: Deborah Tricker
Publisher: Simone Foster
Media Publisher: Sue Ashcroft
Workbook Publisher: Luke Baxter
Content Developers: Stephanie Bremner, Deborah Goldblatt
Editors: Peter Anderson, Lauren Cubbage, Debra Emmett, Siân Jones, Bruce Wade, Charlotte Wilkin, Emma Wilkinson
Editorial Assistants: Emily Ashmore, Jamie Bowman, Shannon Neill, Rachael Williamson
Americanization: Shira Evans, Debbie Goldblatt
Design Manager: Lorna Heaslip
Cover Design: This Ain't Rock'n'Roll, London
Design & Layout: Lorna Heaslip, emc Design Ltd
Photo Researcher: Magdalena Mayo
Talking Zone **video:** Bagley Wood Productions
Audio Production: Tom, Dick and Debbie Productions
App Development: The Distance

We would also like to thank the following people for their valuable contribution to writing and developing the material:
Jake Hughes, Luiz Otávio Barros, Elizabeth Walter, Kate Woodford, Brigit Viney, Louis Rogers, Tom Hadland, Diarmuid Carter (Video Script Writer), Belen Fernandez (App Project Manager), Rob Sved (App Content Creator)

We would like to thank all those who have given their kind permission to reproduce material for this book:

Illustrators: Beach-o-matic Ltd; Victor Beuran c/o Astound Inc.; Roger Harris c/o NB Illustration; Guillaume Gennet c/o Lemonade; Julia Scheele

Photos:
Jasper James; Lauren Demby/ www.laurenreneedesigns.com; University of North Carolina/Chichi Zhu/ The Daily Tar Heel; 123RF; ALAMY/Akademie, David Gee 4, Roman Lacheev, Everett Collection Inc, Collection Christophel, Wavebreak Media ltd, ian nolan, dpa picture alliance, juan moyano, Rafael Ben-Ari; CATERS NEWS AGENCY/Mercury Press; GETTY IMAGES SALES SPAIN/Bettmann, AndreyPopov, wdstock, Onfokus, GoodLifeStudio, Historical, Leemage, Hulton Archive, Marisa9, SuperStock, Remains, Eugen Wais/ EyeEm, Beer5020, Georgijevic, Comstock, Doble-d, Mihiander, krugli, gynane, Darryl Leniuk, Allkindza, D3sign, eranicle, Dutourdumonde, Bet_Noire, Courtneyk, FatCamera, Rommel Demano, Motortion, RossHelen, Bluecinema, SolStock, Jasmina007, Ocskaymark, SHAH MARAI, Hollie Fernando, Tarzahnova, Thinkstock, Wade Davis, IPGGutenbergUKLtd, Apichon_tee, E. O. Hoppe, Edu Hawkins, Jose Luis Pelaez Inc, Hero Images, Hocus-focus, JEFF HAYNES, Aluxum, Per Makitalo, Red_frog, PeopleImages, Szepy, Michaelpuche, Tim Robberts, Mdesigner125, RunPhoto, Compassionate Eye Foundation/ Chris Windsor, Tetmc, calvindexter, BERTRAND GUAY, Caspar Benson, Creative Crop, Rawpixel, Mphillips007, G-stockstudio, Kelvin Murray, Kevin Summers, Monty Rakusen, Olha_Oleskova, Peter Dazeley, Yuri_Arcurs, Slphotography, Steve De Neef, Adogslifephoto, AntonioGuillem, Archive Photos, ELIZABETH

All rights reserved. No part of this book may be reproduced, stored in a retrieval system or transmitted in any form by any means, electronic, mechanical, photocopying, recording or otherwise, without the prior permission in writing of the Publisher.

RUIZ, Flying Colours, SunnySashka, KidStock, Paul Archuleta, StellarGraphic, Tais Policanti, franckreporter, EMMANUEL DUNAND, Frank Micelotta, Orbon Alija, Photos.com Plus, Print Collector, Jelena Danilovic, Jun Tsukuda/Aflo, Larry Busacca/PW, Alex Livesey-FIFA, Artpartner-images, Victoria Bee Photography, PhotoAlto/ Sigrid Olsson, Dorling Kindersley, Oscar Galvan Felez, Stephanie Phillips, m-imagephotography, Dimitrios Kambouris, The Washington Post, Mattjeacock, Caiaimage/Robert Daly, KatarzynaBialasiewicz, Echwan Effendi / EyeEm, Nautilus_shell_studios, Caiaimage/Paul Bradbury, PhotoAlto/Sigrid Olsson, Highwaystarz-Photography, Flashpop, GARO, krisanapong detraphiphat, Mint Images - Frans Lanting, ZEPHYR/SCIENCE PHOTO LIBRARY, SCIEPRO/SCIENCE PHOTO LIBRARY, Ghislain & Marie David de Lossy, Science Photo Library - LEONELLO CALVETTI, Pixelfit, Johnny Louis; I. PREYSLER; ISTOCKPHOTO/Getty Images Sales Spain, Lisovskaya; NASA; PA PHOTOS/Lynne Cameron; SHUTTERSTOCK/Rob Latour/ REX/Shutterstock, ginger_polina_bublik, mimagephotography, Andrey Kozachenko, Syda Productions, TeodorLazarev, eurobanks, AJR_photo; LEXAR; THE BRITISH MUSEUM, LONDON/Trustees of the British Museum; ARCHIVO SANTILLANA; ALAMY/Jeff Gilbert, Alex Segre, Jason Bryan; GETTY IMAGES SALES SPAIN/Izusek, Westend61, Maskot, BraunS, AscentXmedia, Triloks, Grinvalds, Alfredo Lietor, Manyakotic, Paul Burns, Shotbydave, Serts, OwenJCSmith, NiseriN, George Marks, Image Source, PeopleImages, Peter Muller, Martin Harvey, Rubberball Productions, AntonioGuillem, ClarkandCompany, NoSystem Images, Steve Debenport, Frank and Helena, Mypurgatoryyears, Ian Ross Pettigrew, Shapecharge, Vgajic; ISTOCKPHOTO/Getty Images Sales Spain; NASA/NASA Headquarters - Greatest Images of NASA (NASA- HQ-GRIN); SHUTTERSTOCK/Dan Wooler / Shutterstock, Photographee.eu, holbox; ARCHIVO SANTILLANA

Cover Photo: GETTY IMAGES SALES SPAIN/swissmediavision

Texts:
p.7 Adapted from article 'Gregory Porter: 'My mother pushed me to follow my dream'', interview by Sarah Ewing, www. theguardian.com, 16 December 2016, Copyright Guardian News & Media Ltd 2018, reprinted by permission.

p.8 Extracts from article 'Alistair Brownlee: 'Mum wouldn't have been happy if I'd left Jonny behind'' by Eleanor Steafel, www. telegraph.co.uk, 24 September 2016, © Telegraph Media Group Limited 2016, reprinted by permission.

We would like to thank the following reviewers for their valuable feedback which has made Personal Best possible. We extend our thanks to the many teachers and students not mentioned here.
Brad Bawtinheimer, Manuel Hidalgo, Paulo Dantas, Diana Bermúdez, Laura Gutiérrez, Hardy Griffin, Angi Conti, Christopher Morabito, Hande Kokce, Jorge Lobato, Leonardo Mercato, Mercilinda Ortiz, Wendy López

The Publisher has made every effort to trace the owner of copyright material; however, the Publisher will correct any involuntary omission at the earliest opportunity.

Printed in Brazil by Forma Certa Gráfica Digital, 2024.
Lote: 788083